FOREIGN POLICY OF INDIA

FOREIGN POLICY OF INDIA

Dr. P.B. Rathod

Commonwealth

Foreign Policy of India

Edition : 2023

ISBN 978-81-311-0225-1

Published by :

COMMONWEALTH PUBLISHERS
4831/24, Prahlad Street,
Ansari Road, Darya Ganj,
New Delhi - 110002
Ph. : 23275511, 23257835
e-mail : commonwealthbooks@gmail.com

Typesetting by :

Rishu Computers
Delhi - 110051

Printed at :
Roshan Offset Printers
Delhi

FOREWORD

Dr. P.B. Rathod is a great writer. His writings indicates his multifaceted personality. I have immense pleasure in writing 'Foreword' to Dr. P.B. Rathod book on 'Foreign Policy of India'. It is a book worth reading and interesting not only by the students of Political Science and Public Administration, but also the students appearing for Indian Administrative Service, Indian police-service, Indian Foreign Service and other allied services. It is also a book worth reading by the members of Parliament, Foreign Ministers, Prime Ministers, Political leaders, Journalists, Academicians, senior officers of the ministry of External Affairs, Ambassadors, senior officials in key positions in the Government of India.

The book *i.e.* 'Foreign Policy of India' is divided into six chapters. The first chapter highlights the Nature of Foreign Policy. In the second chapter the learned writer explained the Instruments of Foreign Policy. The third chapter illustrates the objectives and the principles of Foreign Policy. In the fourth chapter Dr. Rathod exhaustively discussed about the India and Her Neighbours. He also continued India's Relations with Neighbouring countries in fifth chapter. The last chapter deals with India and United Nations and SAARC.

The speciality of the book is each chapter is followed by notes. And at the end Dr. Rathod has given the exhaustive list of the Bibliography. At the end, I wish the writer of this book all the success in his academic endeavours.

Dr. G. Rameshwaram
Head,
Dept. of Public Administration
and Human Resource Management
Kakatiya University,
Warangal (AP)

PREFACE

The Foreign Policy of India has been prepared essentially though not exclusively, as a text book for Indian University students. The thrust in this book is on fundamental values cherished by our founding fathers in the area of international relations. Efforts have been made to analyse these values and examine as to what extent they have actually been executed. India maintains relations with her neighbours and plays an active role in various international and regional organisations. It was not possible in this work to cover all these countries and organisations it is not possible in this work to cover all these countries and organisations. It is hoped that the book will serve the purpose of our young students, and will be of use to the general reader interested in Foreign policy of India.

Dr. P.B. Rathod

ACKNOWLEDGEMENT

Non-availability of a comprehensive work on the subject prompted me to undertake the present study. But in pursuing this study non-availability of the source material prevented a difficult problem. I had to search out and depend upon a variety of research material recent publications, Journals, reports, diffirent embassy publications etc. On account of the relatively wide coverage of the book, it has not been possible for me to go very deeply into each specific aspect of India's foreign policy, and there is obviously considerable scope for further research on specific problems. In fact, one of the aims of this work is to stimulate such research. I shall consider my labour to have been fruitful if the book leads to further research on each of the problems discussed in it.

I would like to place on record of my gratitude to numerous scholars whose books and articles were freely consulted by me while preparing this book. My wife Vimala Rathod endered very valuable assistance to me not only by procuring books for my use, but also by expressing her views freely on the book prepared by me. These discussions were very useful indeed. Dr. R.B. Gadagimath, librarian deserves a special thanks for having provided various learned Journals and magazines that were very useful in preparing this work.

I am thankful to all those who have helped me in writing this book, particularly my thanks are due to my publisher Ajay Verma, New Delhi whose help facilitated the publication of this book.

Dr. P.B. Rathod

CONTENTS

CONTENTS

1

The Nature of Foreign Policy

The framing of foreign policy is an essential activity of the modern state. In fact, all states have some kind of relations with one another, however, distant one state may be from the other ones. Every state has to behave with other states in a particular manner, the study of this behaviour is really the content of foreign policy. The behaviour of one state effects the behaviour of other states.[1] But every state tries to maximise the favourable effect of the actions of other states which Modelski calls "The Purpose of Foreign Policy".

Foreign policy and diplomacy have been described as wheels with which the process of international relations operates. No state can live in isolation. Even before the interdependence of states reached the present stage, the states had several types of relations among themselves.[2] These include trade relations cultural relations and also of course, political relations. Every state, like an individual, seeks to promote its own interests. These interests are called national interests. Foreign Policy is formulated by every state so as to serve its national interests. The government have to decide on a certain course of action and refrain from certain others. Accordingly, governments behave in a particular manner in relation to governments of other states.[3] As professor Mahendra Kumar says, "The study of this behaviour is, broadly speaking, the content of foreign policy."[4] The behaviour of each state affects the behaviour of others. Every state, keeping in view its national interests, tries to take maximum advantage of the actions of other states. Thus, the primary purpose of foreign policy is to seek adjustments in the behaviour of other states in favour of oneself.[5]

Definitons

A policy, according to Webster's New International Dictionary, is defined as "a settled or definite course or method adopted and followed by a government, institution, body or individual" and it is also stated as a wise device for attaining given objectives. It is also defined as the "general principles by which a government is guided in its management of public affairs" (Law Dictionary).[6] Actually "Foreign Policy is the content or a substance of a nation's efforts to promote its interests *vis-a vis* other nations" (N.L. Hill)[7]. It is a means to the desired end for, as we understand policies are specific courses of action designed to achieve desired objectives. The objectives are interests spelled out and made more precise in the current pattern of International Relations.

Foreign Policy consists of the course of action undertaken by a state in pursuance objectives beyond the limits of its own jurisdiction "A Foreign Policy" writes Hartmann, "is a systematic statement of deliberately selected national interests."[8]

"Foreign Policy," said Dr. Johnson in his dictionary "is the art of Government Chiefly with respect to foreign powers." In Europe statesmen distinguished between domestic policy and foreign policy. The Foreign Policy of a state is something more than a mere collection of the several policies which it observes with respect to individual countries.

"Foreign Policy now is the bundle of principles and practices that regulate the intercourse of a state with other states," says Ruthnaswamy.[9]

Foreign Policy has been defined by Modelski as "the system of activities evolved by communities for changing the behaviour of other states and for adjusting their own activities to the itnernational environment." Hugh Gibson has defined foreign poilcy as "a well rounded, comprehensive

plan, based on knowledge and experience, for conducting the business of government with the rest of the world. It is aimed at promoting and protecting the interests of the nation".[10] According to Northedge, foreign policy is an interaction between forces originating outside the country's borders and those working within them. Thus, the emphasis in every definition is on behaviour of states to regulate their own actions and, if possible, change or regulate the behaviour of other states, with the view of serving their national interests."

At this stage, full implications of Modelski's definition may be analysed. As mentioned above, he says, that foreign policy implies 'changing the behaviour of other states'. This means, according to Modelski, a desirable change in the behaviour of other states is the end of foreign policy. But according to professor Mahendra Kumar, this is an incomplete and imperfect meaning of foreign policy.[12] A change in the behaviour of other states may not always be desirable. At times, it may be desirable to ensure continuation of the same behaviour of others. And, yet another time, it may become necessary to make certain adjustments in one's own behaviour.[13] Thus "The aim of foreign policy should be to regulate, and not merely to change the behaviour of other states. Regulation means adjusting the behaviour of other states to suit one's own interest as best as possible."[14]

In fact, a state's foreign policy comprises of :

1. general assessment of the state's economic, military, and international position,
2. an appraisal of its capabilities in advising, self-reliance, caution, isolation, military or potential alignment etc.,
3. broad principles of conduct,
4. national interests, and
5. the strategies, commitments *etc.*, undertaken to achieve a given object.

In the making of foreign policy, the role of policy makers is indeed important. A lot depends on the perceptions and ideology of the foreign minister who guides the officials who identify the aims of foreign policy and determine the principles to be followed.[15] Today the people and media are also playing an important role Modelski calls the flow of actions from the community towards the policy makers as the "input" and the decisions of the policy makers as the "output". According to Mahendra Kumar, foreign policy includes—1. The policy makers, 2. interests and objectives, 3. principles of foreign policy, and 4. means of foreign policy. He, therefore, defines the foreign policy as "a thoughtout course of action for achieving objectives in a foreign relations as dictated by the ideology of national interest."[16]

The foreign policy may be either positive or negative. It is positive when it aims at regulating the behaviour of other states by changing it, and negative when it seeks such a regulation by not changing the behaviour. Thus to conclude, every state adopts certain principles to guide its relations with other states. These principles are based on interaction between national interests and means (power) to achieve them.[17]

Foreign Policy and Domestic Policy

Broadly speaking, foreign policy and domestic policy of a nation are very intimately related to each other. According to S. Clement, the distinction between domestic policy and foreign policy is misleading. Those who administer foreign policy are the same persons who formulate the domestic policies and after all the execution of foreign policy depends upon the nature of domestic problems.[18] Both are, in short, national policies, and foreign policy is the extension of a nation's domestic policy. As a matter of fact foreign policy of a nation and its domestic policy are related to each other in their principles, problems and the manner of making foreign policy. For example, in case of India and the UK the individual freedom, democratic institutions, social justice are some of the common principles practised in domestic and foreign policies. Similarly, the problems such as war, peace, boundary disputes etc., have common effect on domestic and foreign policy.[19]

From the above discussion, one should not reach the conclusion, that the foreign and domestic policies are identical. They are distinguishable in many respects.

The Aims of Foreign Policy

What then is foreign policy about? What are its aims which various governments are seeking to achieve? The following are the main aims of foreign policy :

1. National Interest

(National Interest and Foreign Policy)

Self-interest is the main aim of foreign policy-makers. According to Hans J. Morgenthau, national interest is the chief aim of foreign policy.[20]

The primary task of policy-makers is to articulate the country's external interests and order them in some scheme of relative importance. The articulation and ordering of interests must be continuously changing through time, but a rough and ready pattern in that case of most states might follow the following lines. At the head must come self-preservation, the maintenance of the physical integrity of the country and the unity of its people to this all else will tend to be subordinated.[21]

2. Independence

The next aim of foreign policy is independence meaning the relative freedom of a country from interference in what it regards as its internal affair, and some degree of power to express and implement an independent view-point on external affairs. It may be that the concept of sovereign independence no longer fits the facts of the interdespendent twentieth century world.[22] Nations none-the-less have an impression of their independence—are aware of how it may be threatened, are willing to pay a high price to keep it.

3. Higher Living Standard

Twentieth century foreign policy, writes Prof. Northedge, has been democratised, not only in the sense that public opinion matters more than it did before 1914, but in that the policy must have something to do with the improvement of living standards as well as with the traditional objects of state craft. There is, however, reason for placing these near the foot of the ladder of interests since it is obvious that in the last resort living standards will, if necessary, be sacrificed for 'higher' national interests, as experience in war time or duling rearmament drives shows. Logically, in a world in which states must prepare for thier own security, guns must unfortunately come before butter, and the practice of states shows that on the whole this maxim is reflected in their policies.[23]

Approaches to the Study

The Foreign Policies of the countries have been studied through different approaches during the different periods of history. It shall be desirable to know about these approaches of study in some details.

1. Historical or Traditional Approach : This approach has been adopted for the study of diplomatic events of a particular period with accuracy precision so as to learn lessons for future on the basis of past experience. In this approach there is emphasis on the formulation of general laws and conceptual framework regarding international behaviour.[24]

2. Legalistic Approach : This approach lays emphasis on the study of foreign policy in legalistic terms. Efforts are made to study the external relations of the states in the light of international law, treaties, constitutional provisions. This approach is mainly used with a view to evolve a better world order. The main defect with this approach is that it completely ignores the importance of social and political factors as contributory elements.[25]

3. Descriptive Approach : This is another general approach for the study of foreign policy. The scholars adopting this approach pick up some specific problems or events on the basis of personal interest or bias and try to formulate theories or conceptual framework, using their own judgement on the weighing of various factors. The chief defect of this approach is that scholars have tended to give some attention to many items without giving full attention to any specific problem.[26]

4. Ideological Approach : This approach has become very popular in recent years. This approach tried to analyse foreign policy as an expression of the prevailing political, social or religious beliefs. Thus, the policies are classified as democratic or authoritatrian, liberal and socialistic, peace-loving or aggressive, enlightened or unenlightened.[27] The obvious advantage of the study of foreign policies on ideological basis is that it can be easily understood by the ordinary citizens.

5. Analytical Approach : This approach differs from all other approaches of study not only with regard to the method but also in regard to its general orientation to the field of international politics. It assumes that policy rests on multiple determinants like states historic tradition, geography, local and national interests, the purposes and security needs etc.[28] A country has to adopt a policy with the general framework of these factors. But all the interests of the state are not of an equal importance. Certain interests are of higher nature and must get primacy or precedence over others which are of secondary nature. The students of analytical approach try to make a study of the competing interests, the power of nations to achieve their interests, the process through which policies are adopted and implemented and the international environment through which policies are adoped and implemented.[29]

6. Comparative Approach : A comparative approach for the study of foreign policies is of relatively recent origin and draws inspiration from the study of comparative governments.

Of all these approaches of study the analytical approach is most popular although in recent years the comparative approach is also gaining popularity.

In brief, one of the basic objectives of the foreign policy of any country is the protection and promotion of its national interests. But it is not always possible to attain all the objectives and therefore the political leaders determine the priorities to be accorded to the various interests of the state.[30] The determination of priorities is essential so that they may be able to sacrifice those coming in the lower priority to attain the one's on the higher priority. The articulation and ordering of interests must be continuously changing throuogh time, but a rough and ready pattern in the case of most states might follow the following lines. At the head must come self preservation, the maintenance of the physical integrity of the country and the unity of its people, to this all else will tend to be subordinated.[31]

The second objective of foreign policy is independence of country. This means that the country should be free within its internal affairs and should have power to express independent views on external issue.[32]

The third aim of the foreign policies of most of the countries is to work for the preservation of the present international system and the various rights and privileges inherent in the system. The state realise that peaceful relations with other countries are possible only if stable international system exists.[33]

Finally, almost all states try to work for the improvement of the living standards of their people.

Evolution of Foreign Policy

India commissioned its first nuclear power station in January, 1970 and made its first nuclear explosion in May 1974 these two significant even brought to India a high nuclear status. India has now become the world's sixth nuclear power. Now India emerged as a strong and influential member in the world power system.[34] Now, she plays a great role in world politics. To understand her status and role in world politics, it is imperative to understand her foreign policy, her position with regard to the manufacture of nuclear weapons and her relations with other countries.[35]

The foreign policy of our country concerns itself primarily with the protection of this country with the protection of its freedom, of its security, of its integrity. In fact, the foreign policy of India even today remains what Pandit Nehru had made it. He said

"It is in consonance with the best traditons of India's struggle for freedom and the striving for peace in which all thoughtful people in all parts of the world are engaged in this atomic age. Peaceful co-existence, non-alignment and disarmament are important aspects of this policy of peace and friendship with all countries, especially our neighbours. The policy includes absention from the use or threat of use of force and political independence of other states."[36]

Pt. Nehru can be said to be the main formulator of India's foreign policy. The period of his long association with the Indian National Congress and his three continuous terms of Prime Ministership gave him ample opportunity to formulate and stabilise through practice the main features of the Indian Foreign Policy. Other persons who have significant influence on the formulation of Indian Foreign Policy are Mahatma Gandhi, Rajagopalacharya, Dr. Ram Manohar Lohia and V.K. Krishna Menon.

Present foreign policy of India has greatly been influenced by Prime Minister Indira Gandhi. Late Prime Minister Indira Gandhi on 22nd Nov. 1976 at AICC Session held at Jawaharnagar (Gawhati) stated in precise terms India's foreign policy.[37]

It was, she said, first to strengthen friendship where it exists, second to create where it does not exist and finally, to reduce hostility to the minimum. Mrs. Gandhi reiterated India's policy of support to nuclear and to general disarmament and non-alignment.[38] She said real peace would come to the world when the differences between the rich and poor nations were reduced to the minimum.

In considering the present foreign policy of our country, it would be well to go back to the pre-independence period in which the policy for free India was gradually being evolved. Among the organisations and parties which counted from 1920-46, only the Indian National Congress, which represented the popular national movement expressed its views on developments outside the country.[39] It made it clear that India desired to eliminate political and economic imperialism and to co-operate with free nations. The election manifesto of the Congress, approved by its Working Committee in August 1936, declared the party's opposition to India's participation in an imperialist war. No party opposed this declaration.[40]

The approach of the leaders of the national movements to world problems was unique. As a rule, leaders of freedom movements are careful not to court the enmity of other states excepting the one they are fighting.[41] In India, too, there was such a tendency and some doubted the wisdom of the National Congress in lining with the Republican Spain, China Abyssinia and Czechoslovakia because that antagonised powerful nations like Italy, Japan and Germany. They thought that the policy of Championiong the cause of the weak and the oppressed was mere idealism, which had no place in politics and that India should ally herself with the enemies of the United Kingdom. But the Congress had an internaional outlook. This was the conditioning we received during our freedom struggle.[42] This together with Gandhiji's continuous emphasis on means and not ends, and his total dedication to non-violence became the cornerstone of India's foreign policy.

India's present position in World affairs is significant. This is due in part to her character of being a big, populous, non-aligned parliamentary democracy and to her strategic position, to her membership in the commonwealth and to the distinctive traditions and characteristics of her foreign policy.[43]

It must be here noted that Pt. Jawahar Lal Nehru was the champion in formulating India's foreign policy.

A few days after forming the Interim National Government Pandit Jawaharlal Nehru made his first official announcement on foreign policy over the All India Radio on the 7th September, 1946. In the course of his address he observed. "We shall take full part in international conferences as a free nation with our own policy and not merely as a satellite of another nation. We hope to develop close and direct contacts with other nations and to co-operate with them in the furtherance of world peace and freedom." We propose, as far as possible, to keep away from the power politics of groups aligned against one another, which have led in the past to world war and which may again lead to disasters on an even vaster scale.[44] We believe that peace and freedom are indivisible and the denial of freedom anywhere must endager freedom elsewhere and lead to conflict and war. We are particularly interested in the emancipation of colonial and dependent countries and people and in the recognition in theory and practice of equal opportunities for all races. We repudiate utterly the Nazi doctrine of racialism. Wheresoever and in whatever form it may be practised. We also seek no domination over others and we chaim no privileged position over other peoples. But we do claim equal and honourable treatment for our people wherever they may go and we cannot accept any discrimination against them."

"The world in spite of its rivalries and hatreds and inner conflicts, moves inevitably towards closer co-operation and building up of a world commonwealth. It is for this One World that free India will work, a world in which there is the free co-operation of free peoples, and no class or group exploits one another."

Again, "We hope that an independent India will have friendly and co-operative relations with England and the countries of the British commonwealth. We send our greetings to the United States of America to whom destiny has given a major role in international affairs. We trust that this tremendous responsibility will be utilised for the furtherance of peace and human freedom everywhere.[45]

"To that other great nation of the modern world the Soviet Union, which also carries a vast responsibility for shaping world events, we send greetings. They are our neighbours in Asia and inevitably we shall have to undertake many common tasks and have much to do with each other."

"We are of Asia and the people of Asia are nearer and closer to us than others. India is so situated that she is the pivot of the Western, Southern and South-East Asia. In the past her culture flowed to all these countries, and they came to her in many ways. Those contacts are being renewed and the future is bound to see a closer union between India and South-East Asia on the one side, and Afghanistan, Iran, and the Arab World on the other. To the furtherance of that close association of free countries we must devote ourselves. India has followed with anxious interest the struggle of the Indonesians for freedom and to them we send our good wishes. China, that might country with a mighty past, our neighbour, has been our friend through the ages and that friendship will endure and grow. We earnestly hope that her present troubles will end soon and a united and democratic China will emerge playing a great part in the furtherance of world peace and progress."

We want to be friend every country so that our circle of friendship may grow and become wide and co-operation and peace may thrive. What kind of friendship is that which envisages enmity with others? We should befriend all and stretch out our hands to all. For this reason our coming doser to the great country, the Soviet Union, is very imporant, but this does not mean that we have drifted away from any other country. This is neither the position nor will it be at any time in future. We have always wanted and we still want co-operation among the countries of the world to increase and world peace to be strengthened.[46] The preservation of peace forms the central aim of India's policy. It is in the pursuit of the policy that we have chosen the path of non-alignment. This does not mean passivity of mind or action, lack of faith or conviction. It does not mean submission to what we consider evil. It is a positive and dynamic approach to such problems as confront us. We believe that each country has not only the right to freedom, but to decide its own policy and a way of life. We believe therefore, in non-aggression and non-interference by one country in the affairs of another, and the growth of tolerance between them and the capacity for peaceful co-existence."[47]

REFERENCES

1. Mahendra Kumar, Theoretical Aspects of International Politics, Agra, p. 310.
2. George Modelski, A Theory of Foreign Policy, London, p. 3.
3. Huge Gibson, The Road to Foreign Policy, New York, p. 9.
4. Cecil V. Scrabb Jr. American Foreign Policy in the Nuclear Age, New York, p. 1.
5. Couloumbis and Wolfe, Introduction to International Relations : Power and Justice, New Delhi, p. 125.
6. Mahendra Kumar, *op. cit.,* p. 311.
7. J. Bandyopadhyaya, The Making of Indias Foreign Policy, Allied, p. 1.
8. Mahendra Kumar, *op. cit.,* p. 315.
9. Bhandyopadhyaya, *op. cit.,* p. 3.
10. Nicholas J. Spykman, American's Strategy in World Politics, New York, p. 17.
11. Couloumbis and Wolfe, *op. cit.,* p. 86.
12. Padleford and Lincoin, International Politics, New York, p. 307.
13. A. Appadorai, Domestic Roots of India's Foreign Policy, Delhi, p. 11.
14. Appadorai, *op. cit.,* p. 7.
15. Jawaharlal Nehru, India's Foreign Policy, Delhi, 1961, p. 51.

16. Speech at Mobile Alabama, 27 October 1913, cited in the August Heckscher—The Politics of Woodrow Wilson, New York, 1936.
17. For a discussion of some of these theories see Pierre Renouvin and Jean Baptiste Duroselle, tr. Mary Ilford, Introduction to the History of International Relations, New York, 1967, pp. 3116.
18. For an analogous and more detailed study see F.W. Riggs, "International Relations as a Prismatic System," and George Modelski, "Agraria and Industria—Two Models of the International System" in Klaus Knorr and Sydney Verba (ed.), The International System : Theoreitical Essays, Princeton, 1961.
19. Arnold Wolfers, Discord and Collaboration : Essays on International Politics, Baltimore, 1962.
20. Bertand Russel, Justice in Wartime, London, 1917.
21. J. Bandyopadhyaya, Social and Political Thought of Gandhi, Calcutta, 1969, Ch. XVII.
22. George Modelski, *op. cit.,* p. 13.
23. George Modelski, *op. cit.,* p. 15.
24. Mahendra Kumar, *op. cit.,* p. 314.
25. Huge Gibson, *op. cit.,* p. 10.
26. J. Bandopadhyaya, *op. cit.,* p. 13.
27. *Ibid, op. cit.,* p. 15.
28. Nicholas J. Spykman, *op. cit.,* p. 15.
29. Appadorai, *op. cit.,* p. 15.
30. Padleford and Lincoin, *op. cit.,* p. 310.
31. A. Appadorai, *op. cit.,* p. 13.
32. A. Appadorai, *op. cit.,* p. 15.
33. *Ibid, op. cit.,* p. 20.
34. Stephen King Hall, Defence in the Nuclear Age, London, 1958, p. 15.
35. *Ibid, op. cit.,* p. 20.
36. *Ibid, op. cit.,* p. 35.
37. *Ibid, op. cit.,* p. 40.
38. *Ibid, op. cit.,* 45.
39. B.H. Liddell Hart, Deterrent or Defence, London, 1960, Ch. XX.

40. *Ibid, op. cit.*, Ch. XXI.
41. *Ibid, op. cit.*, Ch. XXII.
42. Mulford Q. Sibley, The Quiet Battle, Bombay, 1965, p. 35.
43. *Ibid, op. cit.*, p. 38.
44. See J. Bandyopadhyaya, "The Nonaligned Movement and International Relations," India Quarterly, New Delhi, April-June 1977, p. 20.
45. *Ibid, op. cit.*, p. 25.
46. See John Stanley and Maurice Pearton, The International Trade in Arms, Published for the International Institute for Strategic Studies by Chatto and Windus, London, 1972.
47. See J. Bandyopadhyaya, "International Relations as a Communication System," International Studies, New Delhi, April-June 1975, p. 35.

2

Instruments of Foreign Policy

India achieved Independence on August 15, 1947. That immediately necessitated foreign policy making by this country. India became a member of international community comprising sovereign countries. India's independence initiated the process of decolonisation, and India decided to support all anticolonial, anti-imperialist struggles. Yet Indias policy is largely based on her history and culture.[1]

Factors or Instruments or Determinants of foreign policy may be said to be those institutions or devices through which the national power or resources are used for the achievements of the objectives of the states. These may be said to include :

Diplomacy

General Stillwell remarked "A diplomats words must have no relation to actions otherwise what kind of diplomacy is it, words are one thing actions another. Good words are a mask for the concealment of bad deeds. Sincere diplomacy is no more possible than dry water or wooden iron." C.L. Sulzberger pointed out that "there are, in diplomacy four cardinal rules. Rule one is always keep the initiative. Rule two is always exploit the inevitable. Rule three is always keep in with the outs. And rule four is never stand between a dog and a lamp-post."[2]

The existing system of diplomacy first emerged in Europe in the beginning of the Seventeenth Century. Since then it has become world-wide and has become part and parcel of modern government.

Meaning

Unhappily the term diplomacy has no agreed definition. In fact, it is used in a variety of ways. Harold Nicolson has indicated this problem in his pioneering book 'Diplomacy'. In current language this word 'diplomacy carelessly taken to denote several quite different things. At one moment it is employed as a synonym for "foreign policy". At another moment it significes "negotiation" as when we say "The problem is one which might be well solved by diplomacy. More specifically, the problem denotes the processes and machinery by which such negotiation is carried out. A fourth meaning that of a branch of the Foreign Service as when one says "my nephew is working for diplomacy." And the fifth interpretation which that unfortunate word is made to carry is that of an abstract quality or gift, which, in its best sense, implies the skill in the conduct of international negotiation, and in its worse sense implies the more guileful aspects of fact.

We can reject several of these definitions. However, in the present context, it will suffice to note some definitons of diplomacy which eminent authors have put forward. According to Oxford English Dictionary dipolomacy is "The method by which the international relations are adjusted and managed." Sir Ernest Satow in his 'Guide to Diplomatic Practice', defines it as "The application of intelligence and tact to the conduct of official relations between governments of independent states."

Quincy Wright in his pioneer work 'The Study of International Relations' defines diplomacy in two ways. In the first place diplomacy means "The employment of tact, shrewdness, and skill in any negotiation or transaction," and secondly, it means, "The art of negotiation, in order to achieve the maximum of group objectives with a minimum of costs, within a system of politics in which war is a possibility."[3]

Diplomacy and Foreign Policy

Diplomacy has got very close relations with foreign policy. In fact, Victor Wellesley stated "Diplomacy is not policy but the agency for giving effect to it. Both are complementary to each other since the one cannot act without the co-operation of the other. Diplomacy has no separate existence from foreign policy, but the two together form one executive policy—policy determining the strategy, and diplomacy the tactics."

In democratic countries, the foreign policy is formulated by the legislatures. But in totaliatarian countries the council for external affairs determines the foreign policy. The diplomatic agents, in fact, have a very little role to play in the formulation of foreign policy except through sending reports, which they send to the foriegn office relating to the interest and affairs of the state to which they are accrediated.[4] Such reports often constitute the necessary data for the formulation of foreign policy. In capable men acting abroad will make nothing even of the most brilliant instructions, capable men by the accuracy and sagacity of their reports and suggestions can do much to improve the most mediocre instructions and therefore, the responsibility for diplomatic action is in reality shared in about equal degree between the home government and its servants abroad.

Functions of the Diplomat

The question of the functions of the diplomat has been a matter of great interest to the students of international relations publicists and the diplomats themselves for many centuries. Prof. Hans J. Morgenthau observes four functions which he calls "four tasks of diplomacy."

1. First, diplomacy must set its objective in view of real power for the pursuing of these objectives. A nation that forms its goal which it cannot achieve may have to face a risk of war. So, it is necessary for successful diplomacy to try to attain its goal according to its power.
2. Secondly, Prof. Morgenthau holds that apart from assessing its own objectives and powers, the diplomacy must access the objectives and power of

other nations. In this case also, a nation will have to face the risk of war, if its diplomacy wrongly assesses the objectives and power of other nations.[5]

3. Thirdly, "Diplomacy", writes Prof. Morgenthau "must determine to what extent these different objectives are compatible with each other." Diplomacy is to see whether the interests of its own state and the other state are compatible. If the answer is in the negative, then the way must be sought so reconcile those interests.

4. Finally, diplomacy must employ suitable means *i.e.* compromise, persuasion and threat of force, for the pursuit of its objectives.

"Failure in any of these tasks," remarks Prof. Morgenthau, "may Jeopardise the success of foreign policy and with it the peace of the world."[6]

The United States Ambassador to Japan, Joseph C. Grew stated the following functions of an ambassador before the American-Japan Society in Tokyo on November 22, 1938 :

> "He must be, first and foremost, an interpreter and this function of interpreting acts both ways. First of all he tries to understand the country which he serves–its conditions, its actions, and its underlying motives, and to explain these things clearly to his own government. At then, country-wise, he seeks means of making known to government and the people of the country to which he has accrediated the purposes and hopes and desires of his native land. He is an agent of mutual adjustment between the ideas and forces upon which nation act."

The basic functions of the diplomat, however, can best be broken down under the following four heads :

1. Representation,
2. Negotiation,
3. Reporting, and
4. Promotion and protection of National Interests.

1. Representation : The first and the foremost function of the diplomat is to represent his government in ceremonial and social functions such as state dinners, receptions, happy and sad occasions of the government to which he is accrediated. He also represents his government in many legal aspects. He may be authorised by his government to sign a treaty and such like documents. He is also the legal protectorate of the people of his country. He may also represent his government in international conferences and act there according to the instructions of his government.[7]

The diplomat, as he is the representative of his country has to take particular care that neither by his conduct, nor by his talks does he bring discredit to his country. His style of living has to be such as to maintain his proper dignity. In appearance, behaviour and general contact with people, he should be careful not to forget that his individual personality is submerged in that of a representative of his country.[8]

2. Negotiation : The oldest and the most important function of a diplomat is negotiation. Many writers regard diplomats as negotiators. Negotiation is the pursuit of agreement by personal relationship and by compromise. In negotiations personal qualities of a diplomat count much. The duties of a diplomat as negotiator include what J.R. Chids describes "the drafting of a wide variety of bilateral and multilateral arrangements embodied in treaties, conventions, protocols, and other documents of a political economic and social nature. Their subject-matter ranges from the creation of an international security organisation, through territorial changes, establishment of rules to govern international civil aviation, shipping and telecommunications, and the adjustment of international commercial relationship to such particular matters as immigration, double taxation, waterway right, tourist travel, and exchange control. Almost the entire gamut of human activities is covered."

3. Reporting : The third and one of the most important functions of a diplomat is to report his findings to his home government. These reports, infact, are the basic tools of a foreign policy. So, "Diplomats must" write palmer and perkins, above all, be good reporters. Major aspects of the reports include the political economic and social conditions of a country in which a diplomat is stationed. The home government will also be interested to know about the key persons in politics, government, labour and industry. The information regarding the industrial production, the public opinion, agriculture, natural resources, finance, legislation, defence forces and the like are very useful to the home government.[9]

Political reporting has to be objective, factual and carefully weighted. It is essential that facts which might be pleasant to the government at home should not be concealed. The object of a report is to enable the governmet to Judge the situation. So, while the ambassador's judgement should be advanced with lucidity, persuasiveness and vigour, material should be provided for the government to come to its own conclusion. Also, reports should not be merely a collection of rumours, speculations and social gossip, they must be primarily an analysis of political, social and economic trends, based on study and observation.[10]

4. Protection and Promotion of National Interests : The last, but not the least, function of diplomat is to protect and promote the interests of his country. So, his main duty is to secure the safety and interest of his own government. If that safety and security can be won by peaceful methods, he should work for peace. If they cannot be won by peace, it does not follow that he should try by every means to alter the circumstances in his own favour. The best way of furthering the interest of his country is not by trying to obtain spectacular success, but by steadily building up a reputation for firmness, fair dealing, dependability and friendliness. His main duty is also towards his countrymen who are living in a state to which he is accrediated.[11]

Diplomacy Today

The importance of diplomacy is, today, diminished. Many new developments on the international scene in the nineteenth and twentieth centuries have greatly affected the character of diplomacy. Harold Nicholson in his pioneer work 'Diplomacy' has pointed out three new developments which have affected the role of diplomacy. These are—1. The growing sense of the community of nations, 2. The increasing appreciation of the importance of public opinion, 3. The rapid increase in communication.

However, the reasons for the decline of diplomacy can be broken down into following four heads :

1. Communication,
2. Open diplomacy,
3. Personal diplomacy,
4. Contemporary international scene.

1. Communication : The first and the important factor that has changed the role of diplomacy is the development of modern communication. In the former days, diplomatic agents made very important decisions because they could get no answer to questions sent home for months together. Lord Malmesbury once said, "I never received an instruction that was worth reading." The essence of this statement is that when the instructions of the home government reached the diplomatic agent, became useless because of the late delivery of such instructions.[12] Today, the rapid increase of communication has altered the role of diplomacy. Under present conditions, the diplomatic agent can receive instructions in no time, his findings can reach his home government very quickly. As a matter of fact, means of communication have opened a new channel for international negotiations. Now the foreign Minister or the head of the government can make important negotiations with other governments on telephone. He can even neglect the diplomatic representative of his government.[13] On the whole, it can be said that with the advent of the aeroplane, the Jep plane the supersonic and various other means of communication, the theory and practice of diplomacy has changed completely.

2. Open Diplomacy : Another phenomenon which has affected the position of diplomacy is open diplomacy. Secret negotiation by the diplomats was the chief characteristic of the old diplomacy. But after World War I, it was felt that secret diplomacy was a grave danger to diplomatic control over diplomacy. The slogan of President Wilson *viz.* "Open covenants of peace, openly arrived at," was embodied in the League of Nations and later in the United Nations Charter.[14] In fact, it was felt by the advocates of open diplomacy that the people have the right to know everything about the international commitments and decisions which should be publicly discussed and should be subject to public scrutiny.

As a matter of fact, because of the increased participation of the public in the international commitments, diplomacy can no longer remain fully secret. Thus, diplomacy finds it difficult to function with the degree of security on which their power and prestige depended in the past. As such, the new trend of open diplomacy has changed the personal and flexible character of diplomacy and thus resulted in its decline.

3. Personal Diplomacy : Another factor which has resulted in the decline of old diplomacy is the personal participation of Heads of States, Prime Ministers and Foreign Ministers in diplomatic negotiations which used to be performed by diplomats in the former days. Roosevelt, Churchill and Stalin personally conducted the world diplomacy in the Second World War. The meetings of Prime Ministers of Asian countries have been frequent.[15] The foreign ministers of Western European countries, particularly, of the Brussels pact powers (England, Belgium, France, Holland and Luxembourg) frequently meet to consider the international problems which affect their countries. The meeting of President Nixon and Mao Se Tung might have been a source of embarrassment to a diplomat. As a matter of fact, this practice of personal diplomacy has diminished his prestige and value not only in the eyes of the government to which he is accredited but also in the eyes of his own government and people.[16]

4. Contemporary International Scene : Furthermore, the new developments in the world-scene have also resulted in the decline of diplomacy. Thus, numerical reduction of great powers, the tendency towards two gigantic power blocs, fear of total war, continuation of the cold war and increased membership of the U.N.O. from 56 in 1945 to double the number and many other developments in the world politics are bound to change the character of old diplomacy.

A study of human history reveals that whenever there was war, responsible diplomats, realising the horror of war, attempted to innovate means which are believed capable of preventing wars. As such diplomats and statesmen preserve and protect the world intact. In fact, the main task of diplomats and statesmen is to find solution of disputes through amicable means and avoid wars by all possible efforts. Thus, it is beyond doubt that diplomacy is the major instrument for preserving peace.[17] Commenting on the role of diplomacy in preserving peace Prof. Morgenthau observes, "Diplomacy however, morally unattractive in its business it may seem to many, is nothing but a symptom of the struggle for power among sovereign nations which try to maintain orderly and peaceful relations among themselves. If order and anarchy peace and war were matters of no concern to the nations of the world, they could dispense with diplomacy, prepare for war, and hope for the best. If nations, who are sovereign, who are supreme in their territories with no superior above them, must try to persuade, negotiate and exert pressure upon each other, that is to say, they must engage in, cultivate and rely upon diplomatic procedures."[18]

To conclude our discussion of diplomacy we may say that with the decline of traditional diplomacy, the importance of diplomats has suffered a great set-back. The quiet days when an honest man was sent as a diplomat "to lie abroad for the good of the country' now seem to belong to the good old times. Present-day diplomacy is an exacting job, demanding many hitherto unforeseen qualities, with certain occupational hazards. Observing the present day value of diplomats, Lord Vansittart lamented that although the number of diplomats is increasing widely, "they have last stature" and "are increasingly mouth-pieces."

But in view of the foregoing review, we may say that their role is still a great one. A diplomat still promotes and protects the interests of his country, establishes personal contacts with the other government to which he is accredited and utilises these contacts in far sighted ways for the benefit of the country, exercises his skill in analysing and reporting on political, economic conditions and trends to his government and creates goodwill common understanding and co-operation for enhancing international co-operation and confidence among governments and people. However, we must agree with Prof. Schleicher that "whatever the relative importance of diplomatic services today and a hundred years ago, one may certainly conclude that they perform an indispensable function in the conduct of foreign relations.

The Personality of the Statesman

To study the personality of the statesman is very important in assessing the foreign policy of a nation. But it is a striking fact that political scientists have by and large neglected this issue. It is, however, very difficult to assess the personality of a statesman. J.B. Duroselle rightly remarks that everyman is different, everyman complex and ambiguous. In a statesman who shoulders important responsibilities, even those who know him well will find elements in his attitude that are unpredictable or even inexplicable. No one can predict with any degree of certainty how he will act.[19]

In fact, it is difficult to assess the personality of statemen. Having learned as much as one can about the forces that influence a statesman, it may seem possible to explain some aspects of his work in terms of his "temperament". The problem then is find out all about his temperament through the study of texts and eye witness accounts, and through the study of his actual behaviour.[20]

Difficulties

According to Prof. J.B. Duroselle, all attempts to classify human personalities run up against two basic difficulties.

1. The first is related to man's essential ambiguity. Man is a biological being, but he is also a thinking and reasoning one, and finally, he lives in society.
2. The second fundamental difficulty is in discerning the innate from the acquired. Prof. Duroselle says that the acquired personality may come from the physical environment, climate, foods, from certain stimulants or drugs (alcohol, opium) that can basically transform the personality from illness and from social factors—environment, education, circumstances of life. The effect of illness in transforming the personality, for example, is familiar.[21]

Classification of the Statesman's Personality

We can classify the statesman personality in the following manner.

1. Psychological Classification : Lasswell contended that politicians, like other men act much less rationally than they think that they do. The objectives they set themselves may be rational, but there is always a wide spectrum of apparently rational objectives, and the choice among them is inevitably determined by impulses of essentially non-rational origin.

In his 'psychopathology and politics,' Lasswell classifies politicians as agitators, administrators, or theorists :

"The essential mark of the agitator is the high value which he places on the emotional response of the public. He idealises the magnitude of the desirable social changes which are capable of being produced by a specific line of social action. The agitator easily infers that he who disagrees with him is in communion with the devil, and that opponents show bad faith or timidity. The administrator is a co-ordinator of effort in continuing activity. The theorist, too draws his convictions from unconscious private motives. Political prejudices, preference and creeds are often formulated in highly rational form, but they are grown in highly irrational ways."[22]

2. *Classification on the Basis of Characterology :* Characterology appears to be particularly a French Science. In the opinion of Jean B. Duroselle, the constituent properties of the human being, "according to characterologists, are "emotivity, activity and reverberation". Individual are classified as emotive when their psychological and physiological life is more profoundly affected by events than most and most individuals will be classified as non-emotive who are less affected than most. Similarly "an active man is one in whom the emergence of an obstacle has just cut off, an inactive man is one whom the obstacle discourages.

The notion of "reverberation" is more unusual. Any image that impresses itself on a man's attention has an immediate "reverberation" and also a subsquent one. When the effects of a mental datum consciously perceived drive back the effects of earlier data, the primary function prevails over the secondary function, the man in whom this tendency is habitual is classified as belonging to the primary type. If on the other hand, the persistent influence of past experiences prevails over the present disguising it, repressing it, subordinating it—the man must be classified as belonging to the secondary type."[23]

How to Judge the Attitude of the Statesman

After the above classification, we want to find out to what extent the personality of the statesman explains his attitudes in the making of foreign policy. For this purpose, as Prf. Jean B. Duroselle writes, "The best way to distinguish the essential features is probably to try to discover in sources such as diplomatic documents, memories, and speeches—the questions that statesmen and diplomats ask most frequently about the foreign statesmen they deal with. In this way, we can arrive at a simple empirical listing of contrasting types."[24] As such we can classify the statesmen in the following manner as has nicely been done Prof. Duroselle.

1. The Doctrinaire and the Opportunist : Doctrinaires or "theorists" as Lasswell calls them adopt a coherent system of thought and try, as far as possible, to harmonise their decisions with that system. Opportunists, or empiricists, do not cling to any one particular system. They regulate their conduct according to circumstances. Naturally, there are no wholly consistent doctrinaires, since circumstances sometimes impose decisions that are out of line with doctrine, and all opportunists have general ideas to which they are faithful.

An example of a doctrinaire, though a more flexible one with an extraordinary faculty for adaptation, was Lenin-Bertrand Russell said on him that Lenin was "an embodied theory." The materialist conception of history one feels, is his life-blood. He resembles a professor in his desire to have his theory understood and in his fury with those who misunderstand or disagree. Stalin followed the same doctrinaire line.[25]

These doctrinaire types may be contrasted with "opportunists". Men like Lioyd George, Pierre Lavel, however, different they may have been in political stature and moral standards, were similar in that none of them were men of doctrine. Their ideal was continuing series of successes, whatever the nature of success.

As a final example, Pierre Lavel the premier of France under German occupation in World War II, whose flexibility was often akin to servility was an empiricist and an opportunist "irresitibly drawn to facile solution," empirical rather than doctrinaire.

2. *The Fighter and the Conciliator* : There are some statesmen who prefer to conquer states rather than to acquire them as is the case with Louis XIV. There are others who shrink from war. In French history example of the former would be George Clemenceau, premier in 1917-19 of the latter Briand. It is no accident that in one and the same year (1917), Briand agreed to take part in preliminary feelers for negotiations, while Clemenceau expressed the essence of his policy with the statement, "I am Waging War."[26] True Clemenceau sometimes appeared as a conciliator for instance in March 1871, or during his term of office 1906-9, but he was essentially a fighter. He liked to make enemies (politicians were almost universally hostile to him) and he poured out contempt on his foes. He justified his last fight in these terms :

"When a man has placed the whole interest of life in action, he is little likely to pause over unnecessary trifles might perhaps have been capable of turning my back on my duty had not the breath of the great days magically fanned to new and old, ever-burning flame of the emotion of the past."

Briand was not that type of man. If, at first, he appeared hot headed it was probably in the interest of his career to be so. But the same interest and his temperament, inclined him to conciliation. The first great event in his political life was his report on the law of separation of church and state, here was a fighting issue par excellence, and he made of it a work of conciliation. Briand himself emphasised the relation between international conferences and the benefits of conciliation.[27]

These gatherings of people represented by the leaders of their governments are something new in world diplomacy. And even........ if they do not produce all the results which might be expected, they are useful because they can dispel many misunderstandings, they can prompt many endeavours which will bring the people closer together, summoring them to make reciprocal concessions.

3. The Idealist and the Cynic : Some of the statesmen are idealists or cynics. Wilson was an idealist, whereas Bismark was a cynic. "There are examples of this attitude in Wilson's statements at his meetings with Clemenceau, Liyod George, and Orlando. He argued for instance, that U.S. policy was to secure an equitable territorial settlement and a lasting agreement among peoples hence the United States greatly desires to eliminate all sources of discord and antagonism." In other words, the ideal of a lasting peace could be promoted by the application of certain general principles, not by the furtherance of particular interests.[28] The rejection of particular interests applied to the United States as well. What he sought, said Wilson was not to deviate from the path of the world's great thrust towards justice. He wished to do nothing that would allow others to say of Americans that they professed fine principles but made exception wherever sentiment or national interest promoted them to depart from the rule.[29]

Such attitude was never found in Bismark. His "cynicism" was more than rough frankness verbal brutality which he used as a tried and true instrument of diplomacy. It was above all "sacred egoism" and an admission that the state was a supreme value. Yet, Bismark was not a totalitarian. He recognised an international society based on certain rules.

4. The Inflexible and the Imaginative : The inflexible man sticks to certain methods. He is not a creator. He is unable to solve new problems. The imaginative man can invent new solutions. For example, we can contrast Hoover with Roosevelt. Hoover was a President of the USA. According to Mario Einandi "Temperamentally, Stimson and Mr. Hoover were totally different. One was by nature and training an advocate and a fighter the other was an organiser and planner. Mr. Hoover liked to calculate his moves as he would the building of a bridge, while Stimson preferred to choose his main objective and then charge ahead without worrying confident that aggressive executive leadership would win followers."[30]

Frank D. Roosevelt, on the other hand, confronted with the economic crisis, produced (with the help of his "brain trust") flexible and imaginative methods of governmental intervention. Halted in this endeavour by the Supreme Court, he hit on the expedient of reforming it, it was a "Roosevelt revolution." Roosevelt, according to one writer was "the Supreme democratic leader of our time."

5. *The Gambler and the Cautious Man :* Some statesmen are gamblers and they take risks. There are others who avoid risks and are slow and prefer to wait. We can distinguish Napoleon III and Marshal Petain, who for example, combined a certain taste for danger with extreme irresolution in executing decisions. "We should make circumstances, we should let them develop and then adopt our decisions them—The "wait and see" attitude, often the policy of the irresolute. Marshal Petain in 1940-44, who advanced age doubtless had something to do with his indecision (witness his hesitation over whether to choose Baudouin or Lavel as Foreign Minister on June 16, 1940, and again over what response he should make to the British attack on the French fleets at Mers-el-Kebir on June 3), was the very embodiment of the "wait and see" advocate. It was probably a deep-rooted personality trait, "I am waiting for the Americans and the tanks,"[31] he had said in 1917.

Geographical Factors

Is foreign policy influenced by its geographical factors? Does the study of geographical data alone make it possible to define the guiding principles of a particular State's Foreign Policy? What is the importance of political geography in International politics?

Political thinkers, from Jean Bodin to Turgot, from Montesquieu to Michelet, were much concerned with these problems. Many insisted on the importance of geographical factors, Hegel and Gobineau considered them negligible. Some posited a "Geographical Determination"—Victor Cousin, the early nineteenth century French philosopher, for instance, said.

However, to study the significance of geography in international politics, we shall turn over study to examine the four specific geographic factors of size of area, location, climate and topography.[32]

1. Size of Area : The land area of a nation is in itself an element of power. It has an influence on power. In fact, the large area of a nation contributes to its power in a number of ways. A large area can accommodate large population and various natural resources. It may also bring certain military advantages to a nation's power. It helps a nation to retreat without surrendering. The size of area of the Soviet Union, which extends over one seventh of the land area of the earth, helped her to defeat the armies of Napoleon and Hitler in Russia.[33] Similarly, due to the large area of China, the armies of Japan had to suffer defeat in her wars with the United States and Soviet Union are regarded as the greatest powers in the world, because both these nations have extremely large areas. England in these days she was the biggest power in the world controlled a large area of land than any other nation of the world. So, size of area is obviously an important factor in determining national power. In fact, size is an important geographical factor in the evaluation of a political unit, for without sufficient size no nation can ever rank as a leading world power.

Any state according to Ratzal is necessarily in conflict with the outside world in defence of the land it possesses, and any properly organised state endeavours to enlarge its area because this will either bring it more plentiful resources or greater security. Ratzal argues that "space consciousness" is the centre of the theory that citizens of a large state have a "broad" view because they enjoy varied means of existence and great freedom of movement, whereas people occupying a "small space" generally have more timid or modest attitude. He regards space as a 'political force'. In the contemporary world, Ratzal argues, the small state can no longer hope to expand, and finds it hard to maintain complete independence, whereas a large state is often most 'eager to expand'. As a matter of fact, small countries are always handicapped by their small size.[34] Their small area fails to provide space for a large population. Their smallness in fact, prevents them from becoming great powers. Examples are Switzerland in the sixteenth century and Dutch Republic in the seventeenth century. In both these cases small size prevented sustained greatness.

However, it must be pointed out here that larger size is not always a sign of greatness and power. Many states, though they have a large area are not great powers. Australia is a good example to illustrate this point. Australia has an area of about three million square miles, 240 times more than Netherlands. Still Australia is not a great power. It is believed that size is not the only sign of greatness of any country. Yet we can fairly say that size is quite advantageous to a state.[35]

2. *Shape* : Closely related to location and size is the element of shape which is considered as a significant physical property of an area. Compact shape is really an advantage to the state. As a matter of fact compactness has a great value for a state. For example, Switzerland, Hungary and Rumania are at an advantage because of the compact shape of their area.

"Lack of compactness," writes Prof. Pounds is politically significant only in so far as it increases the variety of social groups and physical environments, adds to the difficulties of travel communications, and increases the length of boundary to be guarded." Prof. Pounds believes—It is not difficult to think of countries whose unusual shape has added to their political and administrative problems. Chile and Norway are cases in point. Neither has a railroad which runs the whole length of its territory. Norway has all-weather roads, but not Chile. Both have to rely heavily on a somewhat uncertain coastal shipping and Chile has been obliged to relax its tariff regulations for its most northerly province and its three most southerly. The great west to east extension of Czechoslovakia, coupled with the existence of mountain barriers, has hindered communications and contributed to the separatist feelings of Slovakia.[36] The most Westerly and most isolated province of Austria, Vorarlberg, once tried to secede and join the Swiss confederation.

3. Location : The role of state in international affairs is strongly affected by its location on the map. It is due to good location that some of the states which are small in area have made a greater mark on history than large nations endowed with far greater resources. The geographical location of any state can be expressed in three ways :

(*a*) in terms of its climate,

(*b*) in terms of its access to the sea,

(*c*) in terms of control of transit routes.

(a) Location in terms of climate : Early writers laid more stress on the climate of a country. Plato wrote in the 'Laws'—"We must not fail to notice that some districts are naturally superior to others for the breeding of men of a good or bad type." "Soft countries," wrote Herodotus, "invariably breeds softmen—The Persians elected to live as an imperial people in a rough country rather than to cultivate the lowlands as some other nation's slaves." The early Greek medieval writer, Hippocrates was more precise when he wrote—"The deficiency of spirit, of course, observable in the human inhabitants of Asia has for its principal cause the low margin of seasonal variability in temperature of that continent which is approximately stable through the year."[37]

Such views were firmly held by ancient writers and continued to be accepted by most medieval and many modern writers. Jean Bodin, writing towards the end of the sixteenth century, remarked that "northern peoples excel in bodily physical strength, southern peoples in craft and genius climate being most favourable, between these extremes, the middle people are best adapted to control politics." Montesquieu wrote similarly in the eighteenth century—One should not be astonished that the weakness of the inhabitants of warm climates should make them slaves and the courage of those in cold climates should keep them free. This is a result of natural conditions.[38]

These views are found not only in the past, but also in modern writers like Ellsworth, Huntington and S.F. Markham.

(b) Location in terms of its access to the sea : A second means of expressing the location of an area is to state its position with respect to the sea. According to Pierre Renouvin, Access to the sea is clearly one of these favoured and valuable locations. Territory with a shore frontage has commercial advantages—the sea affords inexpensive transportation facilities, whereas the construction of land routes is a costly business. Despite the risks of navigation, sea-routes ensure greater security in one's relations with the outside world for it is easier by sea than by land to escape from an enemy who seeks to bar one's passage.[39]

These advantages are apparent from Bulgaria's struggle in 1912 and 1913 which was motivated to gain access to the Aegean Sea, Serbia's claim to 'Window on the Adriatic' during World War I, the question of Polish corridor along the Vistula River in 1919, the Chaco War between Bolivia and Paraguay in 1932-35. All these instances and many others prove that the stronger powers try to occupy coastal zones.

(c) Control of transit routes : Another way to express the location of the state is found in the control that a particular geographical location enables to a state to exercise over land and sea routes. Indeed, writes Pierre Renouvin, a favourite theme of political geographers is the constant significance of certain zones of land traffic.

The state whose territory is traversed by natural highway enjoys a special status. All foreigners using this highway must be in its good graces—a profitable situation, since that state can levy a transit tax on the men or goods passing through its borders. And the natural highway can become the focal point around which the state is consolidated.[40] It must be recalled here that Great Britain was long concerned to establish direct control over territories commanding the mainline routes.

Considering these elements, we can safely say that location of a state plays a vital role in international affairs. In fact, it is an important factor in the evaluation of a political unit, for without good location no nation can ever rank as a leading world power. This is perhaps the reason why the study of Geography is deeply concerned with the study of foreign policy of a nation.

In fact, this is an important feature often considered to have an influence on power. It is a major determinant whether a country is a sea-power or land-power. It is often claimed that England and Japan's achievements on the seas have been primarily due to their being islands. Further the location of Germany and the U.S.S.R., one in the heart of the Europe, the other in the centre of the World Islands, brought great land strength to these nations.

Similarly U.S.A., possesses a location relative to land and seas that helps her to be both a land and a sea power. Location has also some strategic importance. The nations located in a strategic spot may have to find this fact a curse. The strategic area of Finland, Norway, and Denmark, *e.g.*, brought war to those peace loving nations in 1939-1940. So, we can fairly say that location is an important geographic factor that may determine the power of a nation.[41]

4. *Climate :* Climate is another important factor which has a great role to play in the determination of a nation's power. It is often assumed that a nation must have temperate climate to be a major power, for it is climate which

conditions its population to engage in an activity necessary for a modern industrial nation. Perhaps this is one of the main reasons that the great powers of modern times have been located in temperate zones. Continuous extremes of heat and cold are alike unfavourable for the development of modern industrial society. Take the example of India.[42] If the summer monsoon brings enough rain the people of India will have to suffer a great loss. However, various claims have been made with regard to the validity of climate, but the fact remains that climate has a great influence on power.

5. *Topograhy :* Like climate, topography is also a major factor in power. The location of mountains, valleys, rivers may determine natural boundaries between nations and as such set limits to their natural expansion. The Himalayas, the Alps, and the Pyrenees mark national borders. Similarly, the Rhine, the Rio Grande and Yale rivers served as boundaries between nations. The natural barriers lying along a nation's frontiers may also help in the increase of the military power of a nation. Thus, the English channel guards the coasts of England and the Atlatic and Pacific oceans are said to provide a natural protection to the United States. But this is partly true.[43] The Chinese invasion of India an October 1962 has necessitated a reconsideration of the question whether topography is important today or not.

6. *Natural Resources :* Natural resources are another significant geographical element of national power. It is often assumed that a nation whose territory is richly endowed with natural resources is capable of achieving the status of a great power. For our convenience in order to analyse the elements of natural resources, we shall divide these into two parts raw materials and food.[44]

(a) Raw materials : A state's military as well as political power is largely based on its industrial power. And industrial power required vast variety of raw materials. In fact, the importance of raw materials is obvious. Raw materials are also essential to keep a modern army in fighting trim. In

1952, Material's Policy Commission, appointed to evaluate raw materials position of the USA and to formulate policies for strengthening it, observed materials strength is a prime ingredient of a general economic strength and growth, which in turn is the foundation of rising living standards in peace and of military strength in war. Military security depends heavily on a vigorous and expanding economy to produce the overwhelming quantities of the equipment, machinery and supplies necessary for modern military strength. On the other hand, healthy economic growth depends importantly on military security to maintain the climate of confidence in the future in which private enterprise flourishes.[45] Neither military nor economic strength can be raised to its highest potential without an abundant and varied flow of raw materials.

Thus, a nation cannot become a great power without having an unlimited supply of raw materials. Lack of oil, which is an indispensable raw material, was one of Hitler's greatest handicap which he could not overcome even after conquering Rumania. The importance of oil is such that Clemenceau during World War I said, "one drop of oil is worth one drop of blood of our soldiers." So, we can fairly say that raw material, chiefly minerals, is the most important factor of nationl power.[46] Today, the Soviet Union and the United States are most powerful nations because they are self-sufficient in variety of natural resources.

(b) Food : Food is another most stable factor of national power. A nation that is self-sufficient in food-stuffs has an upper hand over a nation, that is not self-sufficient. It is for this reason that the United States and the Soviet Russia, being self-sufficient in food, are the most powerful nations in the world. A deficiency in home-grown food has been a permanent source of weakness for India. For, she is always worrried on that count and thus cannot pursue forceful and single minded foreign policy. As a matter of fact, food is a great problem in most of the underdeveloped countries.

Dr. Raymond W. Miller remarks, "Hunger is the most important factor in the world today. The real challenge of the twentieth century is the race between men and starvation." Thus, food-stuffs are very much essential for national and individual survival and for a nation's development in various fields.[47]

7. *Density of Population* : The human element in political Geography is population. It is, therefore, necessary to consider the political geographical value of the population. The best way of Judging the value of population in political Geography is to consider the density of population.

Density is the number of inhabitants living in a unit area of the surface of territory at a given moment. Density of population and political power are closely related to each other. It matters not that other factors such as industrial capacity, natural resources and skilled diplomacy enter into the evaluation of power, numbers of people count too much in our modern world. China for example, which was very weak about 50 or 60 years back, has emerged as a great military power. Chinas man power is really the major asset of its becoming a great power. Similarly India's man-power is the key factor in making India a great nation of the world.[48]

The importance of population has long been recognised population plays a major role in the nation's power. But it is not the only element. Palmer and Perkins have given the following merits of population interms of power.

1. A large population can usually provide more soldiers and more workers and it may also possess certain other advantages.
2. It may permit a greater selectivity and thus a better army, with a superiority in troop numbers.
3. A consciousness of numbers may heighten morale.
4. A population state, through underground activities or passive resistance may better resist a absorption of occupation.

5. Population is also an element of national power if it leads a state to build up its economic and military strength in order to seek additional territory to accommodate what it regards as surplus population.

We can add the following to the above merits—

6. The large population of a country can contribute to the power of a nation in a number of ways. The population can be utilised as armed forces. In fact, modern armies still require large number of men. All the modern instruments of warfare require to co-operate, to service, to transport and so on. Moreover, there is still great need for common infantry. The Korean, Sino-Indian and Indo-Pak wars have proved that there is still great need for foot soldier.[49]
7. As civilians, the population especially if it is large and very thick, may make the task of military occupation very difficult for any potential conqueror.
8. As workers, the population of a nation can help a lot in determining the amount of national production. It might be argued that the coming machine age may not require more workers, but this is not the reality. Actually, in this machine age, more and more workers are required to increase a nation's production by way of operating the machines. The goods that the people can produce can be given, sold or loaned to other nations as a reward for the desired end or they may be with held as punishment.[50]
9. As consumers, the population of a nation helps in determining the size of the home market for variety of goods. A large and good market may encourage the development of home industries. A large population can also provide a large market for producers in other nations. This can certainly increase a nation's power over others. The USSR today, for political ends, gives orders to various countries to achieve its political game.[51]

10. Finally, a large population may inspire confidence in its own people and instil in other nations a kind of fear which greatly helps a nation to exert influence over other nations.

Concluding our study, we may say that political Geography has stressed the importance of Geography in international affairs. According to G. Etzel Pearcy, "War and peace may come and go, but the environmental factors in geography remain relatively constant.[52]

Balance of Power

The concept of balance of power has been in operation since the beginning of the Greek City states. But this is somewhat doubtful. However, there is a broad agreement that balance of power was in operation by the 16th century. In fact, the period from the 16th to the beginning of the 19th century is regarded as the golden age of the balance of power, the period when this complicated international mechanism worked effectively. Late in the 19th century and in the 20th century, however, the mechanism is believed to have been functioning less effectively and satisfactorily than in the previous centuries.[53]

The concept of the balance of power has never been clearly defined. Prof. Schliecher lightly points out, "It has so many meanings that it is virtually meaingless." As a matter of fact every writer has defined it in his own way. Schwarzenberger speaks of it as an "equilibrium". Martin Wright, A.P.J. Taylor and Charles Lerche have regarded the balance of power as a system. Prof. Sidney B. Fay maintains that the balance of power is just an equilibrium in power among the members of the family of nations as would prevent anyonc of them from becoming sufficiently strong to enforce its will upon others. According to Prof. Morgenthau the term balance of power is used in four different meanings—1. as a policy aimed at a certain state of affairs, 2. as an actual state of affairs, 3. as an approximately equal distribution of power, 4. as any distribution of power. Prof. Morgenthau asserts, "whenever the term is used without qualification it refers to an actual state of affairs in which power is distributed among several nations with approximate equality."[54]

The theory of the balance of power is widely held. Palmer and Perkins called the balance of power as "a basic principle of international relations." Martin Wright treats it "as nearly a fundamental law of politics as it is possible to find." It is also regarded as a tool that scholars may use to interpret events and the statesmen may use as a guide to practical politics. For many years this policy succeeded in maintaining peace and preventing any one state from gaining universal domination.

The balance of power is defended on the ground that it maintains the independence of small nations which would otherwise be threatened if a powerful nation were allowed to achieve great superiority of power. As such the balance of power prevents aggression.

Now let us examine to what extent the balance of power system guides the mechanism or mechanics of power politics. The concept of balance of power helps us to measure the relative power positions of nations and also to understand the techniques of power analysis and how it is used and adjusted as bases of action. Wherever and whenever the multiple state exists this concept plays an important part. This appears to be the prevailing notion of all times. The balance of power is defined as checking power with power.[55]

The balance of power is subject to change on account of shifting political patterns and power relationships. It is achieved by intervention and nations that desire survival often resort to war in order to maintain a balance against the increasing power of their enemies. It is a game of power politics. It is meant only for major powers and they are aware of the risks involved and they think twice before they play the role of balances. They often like to maintain the balance rather than becoming parties to the contest.

Recently we have seen the non-aligned countries playing the role of balances between two nations having conflicting ideologies.[56]

The maintenance of independence among nations seems to be the first aim of the balance of power. The second aim is the preservation of peace. The success of this concept depends upon the nation that possesses it. India, for example, believes in peace and considers it a moral obligation imposed on her to protect the weak nations like Sikkim and Bhutan from the onslaught of the aggressive communist China. India possesses favourable balance of power though she has never used it to disturb others and when she was disturbed by others she retaliated with all her might at her command. She humbled Pakistan, and challenged China.

Devices employed for the maintenance of balance of power are increase of one's own strength, declaration of policy aims and methods, co-operative agreements, division of rival power and coalition, military movements, etc.

The balance of power has its own principles. The first principle is that it operates in a general way to keep the average calibre of states low in terms of every criterion for the measurement of political power. The second principle refers to the sphere of activity and the third refers to the purpose of maintaining order and safe-guarding the independence of member states within a given political system. The final principle contends that the balance of power is a universal instrument of foreign policy for any nation seeking to preserve its independence. Dr. Toynbee refers to the aforesaid principles as laws that control the inter-state relations.[57]

Writers on this subject differ while examining the importance of the concept. Some writers think that the balance of power is the ideal distribution of power and a means to pursue a successful foreign policy. Yet, some others treat this as an absolete notion. The instrument that is used to know whether a nation has achieved a balance of power or not is War. War has also upset the balance of power in several cases.

Display of Military Force

The military force or power or strength of a country also determines the effectiveness of its foreign policy. The demonstration of military force is another important instrument through which a nation can impress others with its power. The success achieved by the Americans and the Russians in the space programmes enhanced America's and Russia's national prestige. Since 1945, the most awesome displays of power have been the test of the atomic and hydrogen bombs. Several nations have thus effectively paid attention to their nuclear develoments.[58]

The most important form of demonstrating military force is through mobilisation. The mobilisation of army in the past and in the present by the great powers was clearly meant to show one's own military strength and one's own superiority over others. The Nazis used this very technique a great deal. A state possessing sufficient military strength has greater initiative and bargaining power in the international field. The case of Israel can be quoted as an example. Unlike geographical and natural resources, the military capacity is not a static factor and it keeps on changing. The state try to impress about their military superiority in a number of ways such as atomic bomb tests, mobilisation of army, periodical display of military and naval techniques etc.

Population

The human force constitutes another determinant of foreign power. The strength of a country depends on number and quality of its people. The enormous population of China has enabled her to pursue a forceful foreign policy on the one hand and the falling birth rate in France compelled her to toe a weak foreign policy during the inter-war period. Qualitatively the population should be educated, healthy and possess technical know-how. It may be noted that the population of a state has to be evaluated in relation to other attributes. If the resources of the country are not sufficient to meet the requirements of the large population it poses a serious challenge to the very existence of the state. But if there are sufficient resources for the large population it certainly adds to the power of the state.[59] The instances USA and USSR can be quoted to substantiate this point. On the other hand, if the country possesses sufficient resources but lacks in population, it cannot assert itself in the international field. The example of Canada can be quoted in this respect

Good Government and Leadership

The government and the leadership plays an important role in determining the role of their country in going to play in the international field. Prof. Black and Thompson says, the leadership of societies provides the brain and determines how the strength will be used. In fact, it is the government and the leaders which convert the potential power of a state into an actual power. The quality of government depends on a number of factors—Such as the support extended to it by the population, the organisation of the government, the quality of persons serving the government willingness of the government to take the aspirations of the people into account etc.[60]

The quality of the government to a large extent depends on the type of leadership available to it. The role of the government is dependent on says Prof. Black and Thompson—their decisions will frequently be based squarely on information provided by those who are in subordinate position within the government. Leaders have to decide the allocation of resources and select the particular goals which they have to achieve.

Historical Influence

The foreign policy of a country is to a large extent a legacy of its history. Each country possesses an individuality of its own, which is the outcome of its historical configuration. To a large extent, the approach of a nation to the foreign problems is determined by its traditional values and beliefs which have emerged over a period of history.[61] Though leadership can make modifications of these values and beliefs, but they cannot go very far. The British habit of muddling, French concern with security, the German ruthlessness, the Soviet Secrecy, and American moralism are all the products of the historical traditions of these countries. It cannot be denied that these traits have exercised considerable influene on the foreign policies of these countries.

India's historical development as victim of British Colonialism and imperialism and her non-violent freedom struggle under the leadership of Gandhi, Nehru, Patel and Azad were bound to have a share in the shaping of our foreign policy. Not only this, the legacy of an ancient civilisation and culture also helped in foreign policy formulation.[62] India is too big a country to become anybody's camp follower. Nehru had himself said the two major aspects of our foreign policy, *viz.*, the positive aspect of peace and the desire to promote a large degree of co-operation among nations were partly due to India's traditional values and past thinking. Nehru had acknowledged the influence of India's traditions on foreign policy. He said in the Lok Sabha :

> "It is completely incorrect to call our policy 'Nehru policy is incorrect because all that I have done is to give voice to that policy. I have not originated it. It is a policy inherent in the circumstances of India, inherent in the past thinking of India inherent in the whole mental outlook of India, inherent in the conditioning of the Indian mind during our struggle for freedom, and inherent in the circumstances of the world today."[63]

The traditional values have come down to us from the scriptures like the vedas and Dharmashastras, and the writings of great men like Swami Vivekananda, Tagore, Tilak and Mahatma Gandhi. The three values that have helped shaping India's foreign policy are—tolerance, the equation of means and ends, and non-violence.

Tolerance is the essence of Indian tradition. It is not necessary that views of others be the same as one's own views. To respect the views of others is a great virtue. As V. Raghavan said, "Tolerance is one of the most important, if not most important, among the concepts which invest the Indian traditional culture with a distinction and distinctness." Based on the teachings of Rigveda Mahatma Gandhi had said, "Hinduism tells everyone to worship God according to his own faith or dharma, and so it lives at peace with all the religions." Emperor Ashoka's inscriptions on his rock pillars also advocated tolerance : "The King, beloved of the God, honours every form of religious faith." In our domestic policy, India is committed to secularism which is rooted in the above mentioned philosophy of tolerance. In foreign policy also, India has adopted the ideal of tolerance.[64] It is clearly demonstrated in the famous declaration of Panchsheel signed by Nehru and his Chinese counterpart in 1954. Mutual non-interference as well as peaceful co-existence are the guiding principles of our foreign policy based on tolerance of the views of others. However, tolerance does not mean compromise with our national interest. That is why, after the rude shock of Chinese attack in 1962, India has gone ahead systematically to build an impressive defence system, and having tested a nuclear device in 1974, is in a position to develop a bomb. That is why, India is now known as a threshold country.

Equation of right means and right ends is another important Indian tradition. Mahatma Gandhi indeed insisted on the purity of means to achieve noble ends. He was deeply impressed by Manu's Dharmashastra which lays down—"One should not do a good thing by following a bad path." Indian tradition thus is "To seek to further the welfare of the state by enriching it through fraud and false hood, is like storing water in an unburnt pot and hoping to present it." While the purity of means is the basic thrust of Indian pointed out in his Arthashastra, that what produces unfavourable results is bad policy. For Kautilya, diplomacy was an art, not concerned with ideals but with achieving practical result for the state. He wrote :

> "A weak King, should avert-invasion by making a treaty of peace, or by a teacherous fight in the battlefield. He may reduce the enemy's men either by conciliation or by giving gifts."[66]

This important technique of state craft could not be ignored by our foreign policy makers. Thus, a reconciliation between the "Durity of means" and "reduce the enemy's men" had to be brought about. The principle of non-violence, or ahimsa, was not only an uncompromising faith of the Mahatma, but is also deeply rooted in Indian tradition. Ahimsa does not merely mean non-killing or abstention from doing harm to others. It indicates harmlessness in thought, word and deed, and also promotion of bondless love in the entire universe.

Non-violence is a virtue, though perfect non-violence is not always possible. Gandhiji was of the view that the use of force by the democratic state is immoral. Democracy and violence cannot co-exist. Mahatma Gandhi would apply non-violence to international relations also. The acceptance of non-violent means was to ensure lasting world peace. Nehru took inspiration from the Mahatma, but followed him to the extent that it was possible. India is committed to world peace and has included in part IV of the constitution a directive to the state to seek pacific settlement of international disputes.

The impact of British rule in India and the influence of national movement and freedom struggle is clearly evident in the shaping of India's foreign policy. According to Appadorai, the British rule in India had a three-fold impact on India's foreign policy. Firstly, it gave a stimulus to the national movement for freedom which in turn led to India's support for the freedom of dependent peoples, secondly, racial inequality that existed during the British rule made India realise the evils of racial discrimination and in turn led to India's emphasis on racial equality in her foreign policy and thirdly, India voluntarily chose to remain a member of the commonwealth even after becoming a Republic.[67]

It is not intended to go the ideals and achievements of India's national movement in this work of foreign policy. Nevertheless, it will not be out of place to recall that our freedom movement did not really begin with the establishment of Indian National Congress. It is wrong to assume that the Congress was set up to fight against the tyrannical rule of the British. To begin with it was not a protest movement. But, as the movement progressed from Gokhale's moderate stand to Tilak and Lala Lajpatrai's active demand for self-rule and reached its climax under Gandhi and Nehru, it turned out to be a peaceful struggle for India's freedom based on the Mahatma's ideals of truth and non-violence. Gandhi told Indian people not to hate the sinner but to hate the sin. Most of the leaders of freedom movement were educated in Britain or according to western pattern of education. They valued liberty, equality and democracy.[68] These ideals were valued by the foreign policy makers of India. While co-operating with liberal democratic countries, India did not oppose the socialist countries either. The policy of non-alignment is not only on outcome of keeping aloof from bloc politics, but also in accordance with the goals and ideals of freedom struggle cherished by our people.

Thus, the traditional values and historical developments have had distinct impact on India's foreign policy.

Industrial Development

The industrial development of a state also plays an important role in determining its foreign policy. This is evident from the fact that industrially advanced countries like USA, USSR, Japan, Britain are able to exercise great influence in the international affairs. The prestige of the countries, even the under-developed and agricultural countries are keen to get industrialised as quickly as possible. A country possessing rich natural resources has to depend on more advanced countries for the capital and technical assistance for the exploitation of these resources.[69]

Publicity and Propaganda

Throughout history statesmen have used the device of propaganda to impress other nations with the power their own nations actually possess. However, it is just in the twentieth century that states have established permanent agencies for the exploitation of the possibilities of propaganda to achieve their purpose. Due to revolution in communications, expansion of educational facilities and development in the scientific sphere, propaganda has become a major instrument of the policy of prestige.[70]

Now nations are busy in their attempts to attract other nations to their way of life. Now embassies contain certain "cultural attaches" who use lectures, pictures, posters etc. to glorify their country. The United States Information Service, "tells America's story abroad." Similar is the case with the British Council which performs similar functions for Britain.

In addition to the above methods, nations usually use some other devices also. In the olympics the Russains as well as the Americans attemped to prove that their system could produce athletes superior to those of other countries.

The Soviet leaders have used this device frequently to achieve their purpose. "propaganda," wrote Lenin, "is of crucial importance for the triumph of the party." Russia made good use of the slogans such as "Workers of the World Unite." After their defeat in 1918, the German people were subjected to propaganda that the German Army had never been defeated. Mussolini's propaganda machine was successful and developed many techniques which the Nazi's copied.

Collective Security

The term collective security is a complex one and has many meanings. George Schwarzenberger in his scholarly work 'power politics' defines collective security as "the machinery for joint action in order to prevent or counter any attack against an established international order. According to Prof. Charles P. Schliecher, "Collective Security is an arrangement among nations in which all promise, in the event any member of the system engages in certain prohibited acts against another member, to come to the latter's assistance."[71]

Collective security however, can be best explained in Hans Morgenthau's principle, "One for all and all for one." or in other words, Collective Security is a system by which all nations take collective action against any aggressions which endangers the security of any nation. The idea behind this system is that if all nations agree to take collective action against the aggressor, the defeat of an aggressor is sure and as such peace is certain because no nation will dare to defy the collective action of all other nations.

The relative success or failure of institutions writes Prof. Schleicher, "depends not only upon their quality but also upon the conditions with which they are confronted in the fulfilment of their task." So in the present context, it would be necessary to discuss certain conditions which are essential for the success of any system of collective security. Clerk M. Eicherger says that there must be a largely constituted international body capable of passing Judgement on the facts of aggression based on a previously accepted law. Following the determination of such facts, a legally constituted body must not only authorise but order resistance to aggression. The members of the world society must accept the obligation to resist aggression regionally or universally if called upon. And finally, it is assumed that there must be a collective force, potential or in being that can be used to stop aggression.

International Law

The next instrument of foreign policy is international law. It is used by nations to achieve their goal. In all human communities enjoying government, the rules of law are created by centralised agencies—legislative bodies and courts. But in the international field or sphere no international body has ever been set up with a status comparable to that of national legislatures. As such the international legal system is essentially decentralised. In this system rules of international law generally rest on the assent of the states. States regard international rules as valid and binding only when these rules have been created by the mutual consent of individual states. This is true in most of the actions taken by specialised agencies of the United Nations. Some public international organisations may make exceptions to the rule of mutual consent, the exceptions are few an often relate to less significant matters.[72]

International Organisations

The last instrument of foreign policy is international organisation. Never have the world's people been so anxious to preserve peace. They know that means of annihilating all mankind now exist and a third world war would threaten the very survival of the human species. This mounting concern appears at a time when international relations are growing more and more complex. Under such conditions international organisations meet the real need of preserving world peace.

The idea of international government to maintain peace and human betterment is very old and can be traced as far back as the ancient world. However, for the present purposes we will restrict our discussion almost entirely to the modern world that has existed since World War II. The best known and the most elaborate international organisation in the world today is the United Nations. Its real relevance to world affairs makes it a unique critical force.

The United Nations is a product of the tragedy of World War II. Its primary purpose is the maintenance of peace. Its charter begins by stating that the people of the world are combining their efforts to accomplish certain objectives.

The first objective is to save succeeding generations from the scourge of war, which twice in our life time has brought untold sorrow to mankind.

In the next objective, the Charter declared to reaffirm faith in fundamental human rights, in the dignity and worth of the human person in the equal rights of men and women and of nations large and small.

In the third objective the framers of the charter addressed themselves to the political and legal side and determined to establish conditions under which justice and respect for the obligation arising from treaties and other sources of international law can be maintained.[73]

And finally, they wrote as a fourth objective to promote social progress and better standards of life in large areas.

There is a fine logic in the sequence of these four objectives. The first and the third are based on the prevention of war and maintenance of peace. The second and the fourth reaffirm faith in human betterment and social progress.

The Conditions of Success of Foreign Policy

After dealing with the instruments of foreign policy, we reach our final question what constitutes success in foreign policy? What are the factors which make it effective? The conditions of success in foreign policy can best be summed up in the following three questions.

1. Is the policy based upon a realistic assessment of facts?
2. Is it timely?
3. Is it supported by public opinion at home?

The first question concerning the success of a foreign policy is if the policy makers are working with the most accurate understanding of the situation abroad. According to F.C. Northedge, 'The most correct assessment of foreign situation is of course not merely a matter of accurate factual information, it also requires judgement and capacity to weigh one set of facts against another in order to discern the drift of affairs. Considering the pitfalls in gathering and interpreting information relevant to foreign policy making, the problem is not so much how to provide more and better information, it is the more modest one of how to minimise the distortion of facts to which all policy-making is inevitably prone.'[74]

To proceed to the second question of foreign policy, let us consider if it is timely with the emerging shape of affairs. A model of timeliness of this kind was the initiative of India when she faced a grave and dangerous attack from Pakistan by entering into a treaty of friendship and peace with Russia.

The next question to ask about foreign policy is if it is firmly based on public opinion. In foreign policy, the public opinion cannot be discarded. President's Naser act of nationalising the Suez Canal company in 1956 was greatly supported by public opinion, thus making him a winner on the internaional scene.

Conclusion

From the above discussion, one might conclude that such a policy is likely to achieve its aims if it is based, as far as possible, on an accurate assessment of facts, if it is timely, in the long-run and short-run scene of that word, if it is self-consistent as the nature of foreign policy allows it to be, if understood and backed by relevant social forces at home, if supplemented by appropriate resources, and if smiled on by fortune. But above all, a foreign policy is perhaps most likely to succeed if it is moving with the tide of affairs and weaving itself into the positive volition of other states rather than pitting itself against their resistance.[75]

REFERENCES

1. Jawaharlal Nehru's broadcast to the nation, September 7, 1946.
2. Bandyopadhyaya, The Making of India's Foreign Policy, Allied, 1970, p. 5.
3. *Ibid.*, p. 4.
4. *Ibid.*, pp. 8-9.
5. Constituent Assembly Debate, Vol. 2 Pt. II, 8 March 1949.
6. V.P. Dutt, India's Foreign Policy, Vikas, New Delhi, p. 3.
7. *Ibid.*, p. 1.
8. Nehru, Lok Sabha Debate, December 9, 1958.
9. Mahatma Gandhi, Hindu Dharma, Ahmedabad, p. 8.
10. Implying Peaceful co-existence despite ideological Commitments.
11. Rajagopalachari (Translated by), The Sacred Book of Kural, 1937 Madras.
12. Appadorai, Domestic Roots of India's Foreign Policy, Delhi, p. 37.
13. *Ibid.*, p. 215.
14. Speeches, Nehru, p. 595.
15. Quoted by Appadorai, *op. cit.*, p. 219.
16. *Ibid.*
17. India's Foreign Policy, pp. 22, 43, 73.
18. Swami Vivekananda, "The Ideal of a Universal Religion", complete works of Swami Vivekananda, Advaita Ashrama, Calcutta, 1963, Vol. II.
19. Sri Aurobindo "The Question of the Hour," Bandemataram (Daily), 1 June 1907. The same article was also published in Bande Mataram (Weekly) on 2 June 1907.
20. Camille Vallaux, Geographic Sociale, Paris, 1911, p. 137, Quoted in Pierre Renouvin and Jean–Baptiste Duroselle, *op. cit.*, p. 18.
21. India's Foreign Policy, p. 21.
22. Jawaharlal Nehru "Changing India," Times of India, New Delhi, 31 March; 1963.
23. India's Foreign Policy, p. 436.
24. P. Renouvin and J. Duroselle, *op. cit.*, p. 14.

25. Harvey Leibenstein, A Theory of Economic Demographic Development, Princeton, 1954.
26. Hans J. Morgenthau, Politics Among Nations, Caltutta, 1966, p. 114.
27. Robert Strausz-Hupe, the Balance of Tomomorrow, New York, 1945, pp. 48, 57, 63, B.K. Blount, "Science as a Factor of International Relations," International Affairs, January 1957.
28. J.Q. Stewart, Coasts, Waves and Weather, New York, 1945, p. 163, Robert Strausz-Hupe, *op. cit.,* B.K. Blount, *op. cit.*
29. Harrison Brown, "Technological Denudation" in W.L. Thomes (ed.) Man's Role in Changing the Face of the Earth, Chicago, 1956.
30. Gunnar Myradal, Asian Drama, Vol. II, Allen Lane The Penguin Press, London, 1968, pp. 715-20.
31. Eugene Black, The Diplomacy of Economic Development, Cambridge, Mass, 1961, p. 13.
32. J. Bandyopadhyaya, "Making of Foreign Policy : A Tentative sub-systemic model of South Asia," South Asian Studies, July, 1968.
33. Indias Foreign Policy, p. 79.
34. *Ibid.,* pp. 32, 55, 98.
35. Michael Brecher, India and World Politics : Krishna Menon's View of World, Oxford University Press, London, 1968, p. 4.
36. Edward S. Mason, Foreign Aid and Foreign Policy, New York, 1964, Chs. I, II.
37. *Ibid.,* p. 3.
38. Rabindranath Tagore's letter to a friend, dated 5 March 1921, Modern Review, May 1921.
39. Rabindranath Tagore, Towards Universal Man, Bombay, 1961, p. 272.
40. J. Bandyopadhyaya, Indian Nationalism Vs. International Communism : The Role of Ideology in International Politics, Calcutta, 1966, Chs. V, VI, IX.
41. D.G. Tendulkar, Mahatma, Ahmedabad, 1951-54, Vol. VI, p. 331.
42. Both Bread and Liberty : Janata Party Manifesto, New Delhi undated 1977, pp. 29-30.
43. See B.N. Mullik, My Years With Nehru : Kashmir, Allied Publishers, Bombay, 1971 Chs. 10, 11.

44. Badr-ud-Din Tyabji, The Self in Secularism, Oreint London, New Delhi, 1971, p. 248.
45. *Ibid.*
46. J. Bandyopadhyaya, "The Role of the External Powers in the South Asian Affairs," India Quarterly, New Delhi, October December, 1974.
47. J. Bandyopadhyaya, "The Non-aligned Movement and International Relations," India Quarterly New Delhi, April-June, 1977.
48. Gunnar Myrdal, Asian Drama, Pantheon, New York, 1968, Vol. I, pp. 677-78, Vol. III, Appendix 10.
49. J. Bandyopadhyaya, "Climate as an Obstacle to National Development in Tropics," International Social Journal, UNESCO, Paris, 30(2), 1978.
50. J. Bandyopadhyaya, "Racism and International Relations," Alternatives, New York, August 1977, Ronald Segal, The Race War, Pelican Books, 1967.
51. J. Bandyopadhyaya, "International Relations as a Communication System," International Studies, New Delhi, April-June, 1975.
52. See Henry Kissingner's Speeches on the Subject, Statesman, Calcutta, 16 July 1975 and 7 May 1976, Patrick Moynihan's speech at the UN General Assembly, Statesman 13 December, 1975, full text of John A. Scalis sttement at the UN General Assembly in Alternatives, New York, Vol. I, No. 2-3, 1975, pp. 422-26.
53. J. Bandyopadhyaya "National Character and International Relations," International Studies, New Delhi, October-December, 1976.
54. Ruth Benedict, The Chrysenthemum and the Sword, Houghton Miffin Co, Boston, 1946.
55. *Ibid.*, p. 315-16.
56. *Ibid.*, p. 317-19.
57. J. Bandyopadhyaya, *op. cit.*, p. 30.
58. *Ibid., op. cit.*, p. 35-40.
59. *Ibid., op. cit.*, p. 45-55.
60. *Ibid., op. cit.*, p. 57-65.
61. Harrison Brown, *op. cit.*, p. 35.
62. *Ibid., op. cit.*, p. 45-50.

63. *Ibid., op. cit.,* p. 57-65.
64. J.Q. Stewart, *op. cit.,* p. 68-75.
65. Michael Brecher, *op. cit.,* p. 100-105.
66. *Ibid., op. cit.,* p. 130-135.
67. Hans J. Morgenthau, *op. cit.,* p. 115-120.
68. Hans J. Morgenthau *op. cit.,* p. 121-125.
69. *Ibid., op. cit.,* p. 130-135.
70. Jawaharlal Nehru, *op. cit.,* p. 137-140.
71. *Ibid., op. cit.,* p. 141-145.
72. *Ibid., op. cit.,* p. 145-148.
73. *Ibid., op. cit.,* p. 149-50.
74. *Ibid., op. cit.,* p. 151-57.
75. *Ibid., op. cit.,* p. 158-160.

3

Objectives and Principles of India's Foreign Policy

Historical Background

The foreign policy of a country is determined by a number of historical and domestic factors. In case of India also several such factors have been responsible for the shaping of principles and objectives of the foreign policy. In this chapter we will discuss the objectives setout by the policy makers and the principles on which India's foreign relations are based. Every head of government and his Foreign Minister leave an impact of their personality on the country's foreign policy.[1] Nehru was not only the Prime Minister, but also Foreign Minister for over 17 years which were the formative years of independent India. While analysing the objectives of India's foreign policy, a reference to Nehru appears to be unavoidable, even at the risk of some repetition.

At Cambridge, Nehru had come under the impact of Fabian Socialism. After the First World War, he came under the influence of Mahatma Gandhi and his doctrine of non-violence. In 1923, he had said, "Bolshevism and Fascism are the waves of the West today. They are really alike and represent different phases of insensate violence and intolerance. The choice for us is between Lenin and Mussolini on one side, and Gandhi on the other."[2] In effect, he condemned both Marxism and Fascism. In 1927, he attended the Brussels Conference of Oppressed Nationalities and came in contact with various leftist elements. He developed the idea of close co-operation among the colonial peoples of Asia and Africa. He chose to condemn both British and American imperialism. Later in 1927, he visited Moscow where he was deeply impressed by the progress made by the Soviet Union in ten years. He came under the influence of Soviet communism.[3] His pro-Marxian attitude led to the resignation of six members of Congress Working Committee, in protest, in 1937. But, he was to be soon disillustioned. The signing of Soviet German, Non-Aggression Pact in 1939, Soviet occupation of Finland and excessive use of violence under Stalin pained him greatly, yet he retained sympathy for socialism. After 1950, however, Nehru came to reject communism completely. But, even when he was sympathetic to Soviet Union, he was very critical of Indian Communists for their dependence on foreign guidance.[4]

While in Jail, in forties, Nehru had come under the lasting influence of the vedanta as he got an opportunity to make a deep study of India philosophy. Nehru insisted on being an atheist. He was also deeply influenced by modern European humanist philosophy. He was never a materialist. His personality is summed up by Bandyopadhyaya—"A devout nationalist freedom fighter and the lover of the tradition and culture of his own society, he was at the same time a deeply committed internationalist, and visualised a unified mankind in a co-operative international order, often referred to by him, as the ideal of one world."[5] Thus there were different cross-currents in Nehru's intellectual make-up which, according to Michael Brecher, were because he was unable to synthesise into a coherent intellectual pattern.

As we can say that Nehru was largely under the impact of Gandhi's idealism. Nehru had opined that realism as such "leads to incessant conflict" and that the realist "looks at the tip of his nose and sees little beyond, the result is that he is stumbling all the time." Yet, he described idealism as the "realism of tommorrow," and said that the question of foreign policy ought to be approached "in the spirit of realism." He said—it is easy to lay down principles, but the difficulty comes in when high principles have to be acted upon." It is in this background that Nehru's Government determined the objectives of India's foreign policy which have generally remained unchanged.[6]

Objectives

Foreign policy makers set out certain objectives before they proceed to lay down basic principles and formulate the ploicy. Several of these objectives are common, though the degree of emphasis always varies. A former Foreign Secretary of India, Muchkund Dubey wrote :

> The primary purpose of any country's foreign policy is to promote its national interest—to ensure its security, safeguard its sovereignty, contribute to its growth and prosperity and generally enhance its stature, influence, and role in the comity of nations.[7] A country's foreign policy should also be able to serve the broader purpose of promoting peace, disarmament and development and of establishing a stable, fair and equitable global order.

The purpose of peace, disarmament and an equitable global order may at times be in conflict with national security, sovereignty and development. But says Dubey, in the medium and long run the former may also serve the national interest. The goals of India's foreign policy are simple and straight forward.[8]

The primary and overriding goal has always been the maintenance and promotion of international peace and security. The ideals and objectives of our domestic as well as foreign policy are enshrined in the constitution. India's foreign policy, designed mainly by Nehru, combines national interest with the broader objectives mentioned above. Continuity in foreign policy is a tribute to maturity of a nation and wisdom of its leadership.[9] The objectives of India's foreign policy are so fundamental and generally accepted by the people and different parties that they are known as bases of a national policy. That has resulted in a continuity in Indias foreign policy, "for no government of India can afford to abdicate indepence of Judgement and action and compromise the basic values enshrined in our Constitution.

India, after independence, had to determine objectives of its own foreign policy under very difficult circumstances. Internally, the partition of British India and creation of Pakistan left a deep wound of hatred and ill-will. India was till then one economic unit. Its division created many economic problems which were further complicated by the arrival of millions of Hindus and Sikhs displaced from Pakistan. They had to be rehabilitated.[10]

Very soon the country was involved in a War in Kashmir imposed by Pakistan backed tribals from North-West Frontier. Economy was further threatened by strikes organisd by leftists. The country had to tackle the 'gigantic problem' of providing its vast population with the basic necessities of life, like food, clothing and shelter.[11] Militarily, India was not strong. A hostile Pakistan compounded India's security problem. India did possess vast potential resources and manpower with which it could, in course of time, greatly in crease its economic and military strength. There was another problem. It was related to internal consolidation. Even after British left India in 1947, there were small pockets of French and Portuguese possessions. India's first efforts naturally were to negotiate with the two powers.[12] After prolonged negotiations, French agreed to withdraw, but military action had to be taken, in as late as 1961, to liberate Goa and other portuguese pockets.

International situation was not very comfortable as the Cold War had begun and East-West relations were deteriorating very fast. It is in this situation that India decided that world peace would be a cardinal featu.e of India's foreign policy.[13] India desired peace not merely as an ideal but also as an essential condition for its own security.

Nehru had said "peace to us not just a fervent hope, it is an emergent necessity." As M.S. Rajan said : "For a country like India which is an urgent need of all round development, peace (as much external as internal) is a primary desideratum." It is for this reason that India gave first priority to world peace. As Nehru opined, "India's approach to peace is a positive constructive approach not a passive, negative approach". India's message to the world has been insistence on peaceful methods to solve all problems.[14]

Peace meant not only avoidance of war, but also reduction to tension and if possible end of the Cold War. A world order based on understanding and co-operation would require an effective United Nations. Therefore, India decided to give unqualified support and allegiance to the United Nations. International peace is not possible so long as armaments are not reduce.[15] All the efforts at the reduction of conventional weapons had already failed despite a clear mandate in the convenant of the League of Nations. The problem was further complicated by the nuclear weapons which threatened peace more than ever before. Therefore, an important objective of India's foreign policy has been elimination of nuclear weapons and reduction of conventional armaments. In other words, comprehensive disarmament has been an objective of our foreign policy.[16]

A related objective was to root out other causes of war by measuses such as liberation of subject peoples and the elimination of racial discrimination. In order to achieve this goal, India would follow an independent foreign policy without being any big power's camp follower.[17] It would also require total faith in and support to the United Nations. Thus, pursuit of peace became a primary objective of the foriegn policy. Indias goal of peace was not only directed by its self interest, but also by idealism imbibed from Mahatma Gandhi. Nehru once told an American audience that Gandhian ethics was the cornerstone of India's foreign policy.[18] Emphasising the intimate connection between means and ends, Nehru said : "The great leader of my country, Mahatma Gandhi—always laid stress on moral values and warned us never to subordinate means to ends." He insisted that "physical force need not necessarily be the arbiter of man's destiny and that the method of waging a struggle and the way of its termination are of paramount importance."[19]

Another objective of foreign policy was 'elimination of want, disease and illiteracy'. These are the ills not only of Indian society, but also of most of the developing countries of Asia and Africa. While India's domestic policy was directed at removal of want and disease, it was closely related with the question of foreign aid and assistance. Besides, India chose to co-operate with the various international agencies so that it could make its contribution in fighting disease, starvation, poverty, illiteracy and famine in various underdeveloped countries.[20] Organisations like WTTO, FAO, UNICEF and UNESCO not only benefit India, but India also wants to use these institutions to help the entire mankind.

India has voluntarily chosen to remain a member of the Commonwealth of Nations. This association of free and sovereign countries who were colonies in the erstwhile British Empire now recognises the British Queen only as Head of the Commonwealth, not as Crown of the Republics like India. Before 1949, only British Dominions were members of, what was then known as the British Commonwealth.[21] All these dominions had the British Crown as their monarch also. India did not want to leave the Commonwealth even after it decided to become a republic and ceased to accept the British monarch as the head of state. India owed, along with some other countries, common allegiance to a particular way of life. India considered the continued co-operation with the Commonwealth of mutual benefit to India and all other member countries.[22]

Lastly, India's objective has been to maintain freind of relations with all avoid military alliances, follow non-alignment as a moral principle, seek peaceful settlement of international disputes and promote universal brotherhood and humanism by following and advocating the five principles contained in 'Panchsheel'. India has tried to faithfully observe the ideals of non-interference and peaceful co-existence.[23] All these objectives have been sought to be achieved through principles and decisions of India's foreign policy. Although wars were imposed upon India by Pakistan and China, India has remained committed to pacific settlement of disputes between nations. India has been seeking to pursue friendly relations with all the countries, particularly with the neighbours. India still wishes to work in pursuit of world peace, and in search of that it has been insisting on complete elimination of nuclear weapons, and strengthening of the United Nations.[24]

Principles

A critical analysis of the observations and views of Nehru shows that India's foreign policy possesses the following features or principles. It may be noted that these principles are largely the product of India's traditions and her geographical and historical setting.

1. Non-Alignment : Non-alignment has been one of the basic features of India's foreign policy. The policy of non-alignment is the most important contribution of India to international community. In fact, India was the first country which initiated the policy of non-alignment which was adopted by the most of the countries of Asia and Africa which attained independence in the post World War II period.[25] This policy implies complete detachment from the two military bloc's which had appeared on the international scene after 1945 as well as faith in solving international disputes through peaceful methods. As India was keen to play a dominant role as preserver of peace. She thought it is desirable to keep away from both the blocs. This point was made clear by Nehru as under.

> "If by any chance we align ourselves definitely with one power group we may perhaps from one point of view do some good, but I have not the shadow of a doubt that from the larger point of view, not only of India but of world peace it will do harm."[26]

Further he said that India can play a big part and may be an effective part in helping in the avoidance of war. Therefore, it becomes all the more necessary that India should not be linked up with any group of powers which for various reasons are in a sense full of fear of war and prepare for war. In the interest of self-interest of the country also, Nehru justified a policy of non-alignment for India. He said by aligning ourselves with one power, you surrender your opinion, give up the policy you would normally pursue because somebody else wants you to pursue another policy.[27] I do not think that it would be a right policy for us to adopt. If we did align ourselves we would only fall between the two stools. We will neither be following the policy based on our ideals inherited from our past or the one indicated by our present nor will be able easily to adopt ourselves to the new policy consequent on such alignment.[28]

The geographical considerations also compelled India to adopt a policy of non-alignment. India could not have concluded an alliance with the communist countries because of her liberal traditions India could not reconcile to the ideology which preached open violence and revolution. The Indian tradition was also in favour of a policy of non-alignment.[29] As Nehru said in Lok Sabha on December 9, 1958 that the policy of non-alignment is "inherent in the past thinking of India, inherent in the whole mental outlook of India, inherent in the conditioning of the Indian mind during our struggle for freedom and inherent in the circumstances of the case today."

According to Prof. Appadorai 'the tolerant attitude of India also compelled her to follow a policy of non-alignment. He says the pluralistic outlook of the Indian mind has made the Indian people react instinctively against communism and its claim to be sole truth.[30]

It may be noted that the policy of non-alignment does not imply that friendly co-operation with other countries is not possible. In fact, while pursuing this policy, India established friendly relations with other countries and concluded numerous aggrements for economic, cultural and political co-operation. Non-alignment is also not to be equated with neutrality which comes into operation only during the times of war. A country which follows a policy of neutrality has no positive opinions on the issues which divide the blocs.[31] But as India has freely spoken on the various international issues, especially those relating to war and peace, her policy cannot be described as neutral. This distinction was brought out by Pt. Nehru very forcefully thus : Some people use the word Neutral in regard to India's foreign policy. I do not like that word at all, having myself been in the past, perhaps even now to some extent, not exactly a negative individual, but a positive individual working for positive causes, working with all the vigour and strength that I could command for those causes.[32] On another occasion he said, the use of word 'Neutral' to describe India's foreign policy is wrong except in terms of war. If you say there is a war on today we are neutral. If you say there is a Cold War, we are certainly neutral. The Cold War is in some ways worse than a shooting war, worse not in disaster but in the sense that it is more degrading and it lowers the standards all the time. We do not propose to join that war. It does not matter who is right and who is wrong. We will not join in this exhibition of mutual abuse, because we do not serve anybody that way, certainly not the cause of peace.[33]

It is a matter of common knowledge that India condemned the North Korean aggression against South Korea in 1950, British and French invasion on Suez in 1956 as well, Soviet interference in Hungary 1956, later she even condemn U.S. use of force in Vietnam.

In brief, immediately after the hostilities ended in the Second World War a new and unprecedented tension developed between the erstwhile friends and allies. The acute state of tension came to be called the Cold War. The division of the world into two blocs led by the United States and the former Soviet Union respectively caused the Cold War. India made up its mind not to join any of the power blocs.[34] India's decision to follow an independent foreign policy was dictated essentially by its national interest, and also by its belief in moral value attached to the ideal of friendship among all and pursuit of world peace. India had decided to devote its energies to its economic development. For that, India needed not only friendship with neighbours and big powers, but also economic assistance from different quarters. India made it clear that it would reserve the right to freely express its opinion on international problem.[35] If it would join any of the power bloc's then it will lose this freedom.

Thus, it is enough to say that India is not to join any power bloc—Russian or American. She is to remain aloof from them. She too has to adopt non-involvement in the Cold War. India's foreign policy is aimed primarily at preventing world tension.[36] So, non-alignment is the most important pillar of our foreign policy.

2. *Fight Against Colonialism and Imperialism :* Another basic principle of India's foreign policy has been its anti-colonial and anti-imperialist stand. The Government of India has always championed the cause of the exploited nation against the colonial powers. Anti-colonialism and anti-imperialism has been a matter of faith with India's foreign policy makers.[37] This anti-colonial and anti-imperialist stand of India was partly due to the fact that she had suffered or victimised at the hands of British imperialism and did not want other countries of Asia and Africa to undergo similar suffering. While speaking before the UN General Assembly on 3rd November 1948, Pandit Jawaharlal Nehru said—Asia

till recently was largely a prey to imperial domination and colonialism, a great part of it is free today, part of it still remains unfree and it is an astonishing thing that any country should still venture to hold and to set forth this doctrine of colonialism whether it is under direct rule or whether it is indirectly maintained in some form or another.[38] We, in Asia who have ourselves suffered all these evils of colonialism and imperial domination, have committed ourselves inevitably to freedom of other colonial countries. There are neighbouring countries of our's in Asia with whom we are intimately allied. We look to them with sympathy, we look at their struggle with sympathy.[39] Any power great or small, which in that way prevents the attainment of the freedom of these peoples does an ill-turn to world peace. Great countries like India who have passed out of that colonial stage do not conceive it possible that other countries should remain under the yoke of colonial rule.[40]

Pandit Nehru always insisted on adopting an anti-colonial stand unmindful of the consequences. He said "we are not citizens of a weak or mean country and I think it is foolish for us to get frightened, even from a military point of view of the greatest of the powers today. Not that I delude myself about what can happen to us if a great power in a military sense goes against us.[41] I have no doubt it can injure us. But after all in the past, as a national movement, we opposed one of the greatest of the world powers. We opposed it in a particular way and in a large measure succeeded in that way and I have no doubt that if the worse comes to the worst and in a military sense we cannot meet these great powers, it is far better for "to fight in our own way than submit to them and lose all the ideals we have."

This anti-colonial stand of India was not confined to mere pronouncements. The Government of India gave a practical shape to these ideas as well. Thus, it extended support to Indonesia against the Dutch government. India played a great role in the achievement of independence by Indonesia.

The part played by India in the independence of Indonesia was recognised by Dr. Ali Sastroamid JoJo, the Prime Minister of Indonesia, in these words : "The assistance which India has given so fully and whole-heartedly to my people will be written in letters of shining gold in the pages of the history of free Indonesia."[42]

Libya also owes its independence to India. India also supported the cause of independence in Palestine, Tunisia, Algeria, Morocco etc. It strongly opposed the moves of South Africa to incorporate the territories of South-West Africa into her Union. Recently, India also extended full support to the people of East Pakistan in their struggle against Pakistan and war largely instrumental in the establishment of an independent nation of Bangla Desh.[43] Thus, India supported whole-heartedly the people of Bangla Desh in their struggle for freedom. It is only due to Indias help that Bangla Desh could get independence.

3. Opposition to Racial Discrimination : Another principle of India's foreign policy is that she is opposed to any racial discrimination. India firmly believes in equality of all human beings. It's policy is aimed at opposition to all forms of racial discrimination. South Africa was the worst example of racial discrimination against and exploitation of the coloured peoples including the people of Indian origin.[44] India gave full support to the cause of victims of racial discrimination. Not only India had cut off diplomatic relations with South Africa in 1947, but also used her influence (later) in the application of comprehensive sanctions against the white minority racist regime of South Africa. India did not allow any facility to the racist regime, opposed the system both inside and outside the United Nations and stood by the demand of racial equality. Even Indian sportsmen and players of games like cricket fully boycotted racial discrimination and its symbol South Africa.[45] It is only in early 1994 that aparthied was finally given up and a majority government was duly elected and installed under the leadership of Nelson Mandela. Having achieved the goal of racial equality in South Africa, India re-established full relations with that country. India has consistently supported the establishment of an egalitarian human society in which discrimination based on colour, race, class etc. does not exist.[46] India firmly believes that racialism is one of the sources of conflict in the world, and therefore, a threat to international peace and security.

India has consistenly raised the question of the treatment of the people of Indian origin in the union of South Africa and severely condemned the policy of racial segregation followed by the government of South Africa. In 1952, India alongwith twelve other Asian and African states raised the issue of apartheid (policy of racial discrimination) being practised by the Government of South Africa. India has taken the plea that racial discrimination not only constitutes a flagrant violation of the basic rights or principles of human rights and fundamental freedoms enshrined in the U.N. Charter, but also constitutes a serious threat to international peace.[47]

Condemning the policy of racial discrimation Jawahar Lal Nehru said "we repudiate utterly the Nazi doctrine of racialism wheresoever and in whatsoever form it may be practised. We seek no discrimation of other nations and we claim no privileged position over other people. But we do claim equal and honourable treatment of our people wherever they may go and we cannot accept any discrimation against them.[48]

It may be noted that India has opposed the policy of racial discrimination not only against the Indian subjects, but also took up the cause of Negros in the United States, and non-white population in Rhodesia. In short, India has acted as the champion of racial equality and taken strong cudgles at the United Nations the policy of racial discrimination.[49]

4. Peaceful Settlement of International Disputes : Disputes among the nations are unavoidable. There can be only two methods of settling international disputes—war or peaceful settlement. War has been the most commonly used method of deciding disputes from the pre-historic days till now. War was considered the legitimate means of deciding dispute. It resulted in the victory of one nation over the other. By the end of First World War, destructiveness of this method had reached horrowing heights.[50] Since then it has been increasingly realised by international community that peaceful settlement of disputes should be the goal of not only international organisation, but also of all states.

India has always held faith in peaceful methods for the settlement of international disputes. India has believed that peace cannot be promoted by creating positions of strength by military alliances (which only increase the possibilities of war) but by avoiding use of force.[51] It has favoured peaceful methods like direct negotiations, mediation, conciliation, arbitration, discussions, accommodation and judicial decisions etc. for settlement or disputes. India played a positive role in the resolution of Korean and Indo-China conflicts.[52] It may be noted that India has been a strong supporter of the United Nations as well as has expressed full faith in its capacity to settle the disputes. It was precisely out of this faith that India took the issue of Kashmir to the United Nations.[53] India also extended full support to Indo-China. In the United Nations India uphold the stand on various issues on the basis of merit and has infused to blindly support one bloc or the other. The chief motivating force with India has been the cause of world peace. India has always extended full support to the United Nations in the implementation of its decisions by providing military and other personnel. For example, India sent a number of persons for the observation group in Lebanon which was established by the UN with a view to ensure that there was no infiltration of personnel or supply of arms or other material across. The Labanese border.[54] During the

Congolese conflict also India made available large number of contingents to preserve peace in the region. The valuable co-operation extended by India to the UN was acknowledged by the UN Secretary General Hammarskjold in mark 1959 in these words—"I would like to (acknowledge with gratitude) the co-operation of the Indian people and the Indian Government first of all in the Gaza operation with a very quick response, with a very noble response because Indian units in the Gaza were of a very, very quality.[55] I can speak from personal experience and I am not flattering you. Both of these contributions are very very valuable contributions to the whole development of the UN Security and legal system on which it is possible to build the future."[56]

5. Panch-Sheela : Another feature of India's foreign policy is her belief in Panch-sila. The word Panch-sila came from two sanskrit words "panch" meaning five and sila or sheela meaning "Rule of conduct."[57] The five ideals known as panch-sila are as follows—

1. Faith in one's people—nationalism—without which no nation can be the basis of national endeavour.
2. Faith in humanity which must be the basis of all international relations, considering the case of one's own people against the broad background of the universal brotherhood of man.
3. Faith in freedom which is the basis of democracy freedom of mind, body and spirit.
4. Faith in social justice or equal opportunity for all citizens of a democratic society without any special privileges for any one.
5. Faith in God—as the people of Indonesia, whether Muslims or Christians or Hindus or Buddhists, all believe in the existence of an ultimate reality behind life.[58]

The Panch-sila of Nehru was first embodied in a treaty signed by India and China on the issue of Tibet on 29th

May, 1954. The five principles mentioned therein are as follows :

1. Mutual respect for each other's territorial integrity and sovereignty.
2. Non-aggression.
3. Non-interference in another's domestic affairs.
4. Mutual benefit and equality.
5. Peaceful co-existence.

Faith in these principles were expressed on the ocassion of Bandung Conference held in 1955. In addition of these principles, certain new principles were also enunciated. These includes :

1. Respect for fundamental rights.
2. Right to defend signly as well as collectively.
3. Joining of the pacts without any external pressure.
4. Participation in secret pacts for the sake of benefit.
5. Settlement of disputes peacefully, and
6. Respect for justice.

India continued to adhere to these principles despite a rude shock conducted to her by China by launching an aggression against her in 1962.

The term Panch-sheel soon became popular that Nehru called it an "international coin." The term panch-sheel is found in ancient Buddhist literature and refers to five principles of good conduct of the individuals. These are truth, non-violence, celibacy, refrain from drinking and vow not to steal.[59]

The most important aspect of panchsheel, is peaceful co-existence. Ideology has often caused tensions, conflicts and wars. Thus, Fascism, Nazism played havoc by advocating anti-semitism, ultra-nationalism, war rearmament and opposition to communism.[60] Hatred was spread in the name of ideology, anti-commitern pact concluded, aggressions and annexations took place. The ideology of Soviet Union supported anti-Fascist popular Fronts. The idea of peaceful co-existence is morally so correct that it allows all countries to follow their ideology without interfering in internal affairs of the other. Despite the 1962 border war, India has remained firmly committed to the principles of Panch-sheel.[61]

6. Bias in Favour of Asia : Sixthly, though India believes in the policy of co-operation, friendship and co-existence with all the countries of the world, she has a special bias towards the countries of Asia and Africa. Ever since the attainment of independence, India has tried to develop close-relations with the Afro-Asian countries and has shown keen interest in their economic development. With a view to forge some sort of unity amongst the states of Asia and Africa, India took initiative in organising two conferences at Delhi in 1947 and 1949.[62] Pandit Nehru justified his special interest in the countries of Asia in the course of his address to Asian Relations Conference held in March 1947. He said—"In this crisis in the world history, Asia will necessarily play a vital role." The countries of Asia can no longer be used as pawns by others. They are bound to have their own politics in world affairs.[63] Europe and America have contributed very greatly to human progress and for that we must yield them praise and honour and learn from them many lessons they have to teach. But the west has also driven us into wars and conflicts without number and even now, the days after a terrible war there is talk of further war in the atomic age that is open to us.[64] In this atomic age Asia will have to function effectively in the maintenance of peace. Indeed there can be no peace unless Asia plays her part. There is today conflict in many countries and all of us in Asia are fully aware of our own troubles. Nonetheless the whole spirit and outlook of Asia are peaceful and the emergence of Asia in the world affairs will be powerful influence on World Peace.[65]

Though Nehru had a special bias for Asia, he was not interested in creating a separate Asian bloc. Due to the initiative taken by India in convening conference of Asian countries in New Delhi, it was alleged in certain quarters that India was trying to assume leadership of South East Asia.[66] It was also argued that India wanted to create new channels parallel to United Nations. However, these allegations were denied by Pt. Nehru. He said "We meet in no spirit of hostility to any nation or group of nations, but in an endeavour to promote peace through the extension of freedom. We meet security not supplant that body. He assured America and other countries of Europe. "We have not designs against anybody, our's is a great design of promoting peace and progress all over the world. We propose to stand on our feet and co-operate with all others who are prepared to co-operate with us."[67]

According to the Times of London, Mr. Nehru has sometimes been accused of aiming at the leadership of South-Asia. He has always disclaimed any such ambition. Yet, simple observation shows that this leadership, however, unsought it may be by Indians themselves, is now a factor to be reckoned with in international affairs. In the United Nations, the representatives of Ceylon, Burma, Indonesia and sometimes Siam keep in close touch with the Indian colleagues and are reluctant to oppose their views.[68] The growing tendency of India to speak not for herself alone, but as the representative of the Asian group has lately been illustrated by the part she has played in the formation of the Arab-Asiatic bloc. In part no doubt, India's prominence as the spokesman of the Asian point of view is due to the vigour with which she has taken up the claims of the New Asian national movements in their dealings with the Western World. But it is significant that the Asian countries which are most closely associated with her are precisely those which own the foundation of their civilisation to the culture to which they learnt from her.[69]

7. Close Relations with Commonwealth : India has always sought to develop close relations with the Commonwealth of Nations even though India decided to become a Sovereign Democratic Republic. The Indian leaders decided to continue her intimate connections with the Commonwealth. India's decision to adopt Republican system and still continue as a member of the Commonwealth led to the creation of New Commonwealth which was multi-racial, multi-cultural. India decided to join the Commonwealth because of the numerous economic benefits which she could expect from its membership.[70] Explaining the reasons which promoted India to become member of the Commonwealth, Pandit J. Nehru said "We have chosen to stay in the Common-wealth because we did not want to live in isolation and because it confers on us benefits which do not take away our sovereign status. Again, there is no law behind the Common- wealth. It has not even the formality which normally accompanies treaties. It is an agreement by free will to be determined by free will."[71] In the subsequent years, India continued to take keen interest in the activities of the Commonwealth and develop mutual co-operation with the member countries.

8. Support to the United Nations : India is one of the founder member of the United Nations, and many of its specialised agencies. It has full faith in the international organisations and agencies. India firmly believes in international peace and security. India does not support the nuclear weapons, wants their elimination and considerable reduction of conventional weapons and armed forces.[72] India believes that these goal can be achieved by strengthening the United Nations. India is an important member of the group of Non-Aligned in the United Nations. She is also a prominent Afro-Asian member of the world body. India has sponsored and supported several progressive measures in the UN and its agencies. India's Mrs. Vijay Lakshmi Pandit was elected President of the General Assembly in 1953. India has been a non-permanent member of the Security Council for a number of terms. Her contribution in the cause of world peace has been universally recognised.

India has continuously supported the efforts for the universalisation of the United Nations. There are several areas in which India has played significant role in the United Nations. For example, India has played a consistently positive and energetic role in arms control and disarmament. In the field of human rights, the issues which attracted India's attention quite early were racial discrimination and colonialism (as already discussed). India's contribution has also been significant in the areas of health, food, children's welfare and improvement of the conditions of working people.[73]

9. The Gujral Doctrine : This doctrine is expression of the foreign policy initiated by I.K. Gujral, the Foreign Minister in Deve Gowda Government which assumed office in June 1996. Gujral himself later became Prime Minister. The essence of Gujral Doctrine is that being the largest country in South Asia, India decided on extension of unilateral concessions to neighbours in the sub-continent. Gujral advocated people to people contacts, particularly between India and Pakistan, to create an atmosphere that would enable the countries concerned to sort out their differences amicably or peacefully. It is in pursuance of this policy that the late in 1996 India concluded an agreement with Bangladesh on sharing of Ganga Waters. Gujral Doctrine was vigorously pursued when India unilaterally announced in 1997 several concessions to Pakistan tourists, particularly the elder citizens and cultural groups in regard to visa fees and police reporting.[74]

The Gujral Doctrine, summed up in one sentence as, the policy of giving unilateral concessions to neighbours and promoting people to people contact, is aimed at improving relations by friendly gestures. The Doctrine presents India as a big country willing to unilaterally help the smaller neighbours. However, the Gujral Doctrine was generally welcomed and appreciated not only within the country, but also by most of the neighbours and major powers. In the context of changed international environment in post-cold war world Gujral Doctrine become a new and important principle of India's foreign policy.

Criticisms

The foreign policy of India has met with severe criticism at the hands of critics. Some of the points of criticism are as follows :–

Firstly, it is said that the foreign policy of India is unrealistic and lays too much emphasis on idealism.

Secondly, the policy of non-alignment adopted by India has also been made the target of criticism. It is argued that in a world divided into two hostile camps, India stands aloof and cannot depend on outside help in case of need. As a result of this policy India was looked upon with suspicion by both the great powers and they were reluctant to offer her assistance. On the other hand, Pakistan by closely aligning herself receive enormous amounts by way of assistance from United States and other western countries. However, this criticism is not quite valid because in the later years India received assistance from both the super-powers.

Thirdly, the decision of India to maintain close connections with the Commonwealth has also been subjected to criticism. The critics argue that the membership of Commonwealth has not only curtailed the sovereignty of the country but also impinged on the right of India to pursue an independent foreign policy. However, this criticism is ill-famded commonwealth is a voluntary association and India chosen to become its member because she expected certain benefits from this membership. As Commonwealth is a voluntary association and India assumed its membership by choice, she retains the freedom to leave the Commonwealth any time she desires. Membership of the Commonwealth does not in any way infringe on the sovereignty of India and she can leave it any time she deems necessary. She continues to be its member only because it provides her certain benefits.

Fourthly, the foreign policy of India has completely ignored importance of power in international politics as laid emphasis on settlement of international disputes through peaceful methods like negotiations. It is argued by the critics that these methods can be effective only if they are backed by power. In the absence of power no country would be willing to trust the other and leave its fate in the hands of the negotiator or mediator. The supports of India's foreign policy are not willing to agree with the critics and hold that the doctrine of power is not applicable in the present context when the world is divided into two camps headed by the USA and Soviet Union.

Finally, it is argued that Indian foreign policy has failed to secure the national interest. The Kashmir issue still continues to hang in the United Nations without any solution in sight.

But probably, the most important achievement of India's foreign policy has been the valuable contribution towards the promotion of World Peace. India has not only popularised the peaceful methods for the settlement of disputes but also played an active role in the reduction of tension by assuming responsibilities in Korea, Vietnam, Cambodia etc. While in Korea India took up enormous responsibilities as Chairman of the Neutral nations.[75]

REFERENCES

1. Collection of Nehru's speeches, 1950, p. 4.
2. Bandyopadhyaya, The Making of India's Foreign Policy, Allied, 1970, p. 231.
3. Muchkund Dubey, India's Foreign Policy in the Evolving Global Order, in International Studies, April-June, 1993, p. 117.
4. *Ibid.*
5. K.P. Karunakaran, pp. 22-23.
6. Nehru, Inside America, Delhi, p. 34.
7. See V.N. Khanna, International Relations, Vikas, New Delhi, p. 27.

8. M.S. Rajan, Studies in India's Foreign Policy, New Delhi, p. 27.
9. Quoted by M.S. Rajan, *op. cit.,* p. 27.
10. V.N. Khanna, *op. cit.*
11. Satish Kumar, Towards A Stronger and More Democratic United Nations—India's Role in International Studies, April-June, 1993, p. 188.
12. M.S. Rajan, *op. cit.,* p. 21.
13. Michael Brecher, Nehru, A Political Biography, Oxford University Press, London, 1959, p. 315.
14. *Ibid.,* p. 393.
15. *Ibid.,* pp. 435, 436.
16. *Ibid.,* pp. 564-65.
17. J.S. Bright (ed.) Before and After Independence (collection of Jawaharlal Nehru's speeches, 1922-50), New Delhi, 1950, p. 4.
18. Michael Brecher, *op. cit.,* p. 601.
19. India's Foreign Policy, pp. 34, 51, 73.
20. *Ibid.,* p. 28.
21. *Ibid.,* author's italics.
22. *Ibid.,* p. 443.
23. Sisir Gupta, Kashmir : A study in India-Pakistan Relations, Asia Publishing House, Bombay, 1966, p. 123.
24. Alan Campbell-Johnson, Mission with Mountbatten, London, 1951, diary dated 28 October, 1947, See also Indias Foreign Policy, p. 445.
25. Indias Foreign Policy, pp. 445, 451, authors italics.
26. *Ibid.,* p. 451.
27. Goodrich and Hambro, Charter of the United Nations, London 1949, pp. 249-52.
28. Sisir Gupta, *op. cit.,* pp. 140-43.
29. India's Foreign Policy, pp. 452-455.
30. Sisir Gupta, *op. cit.,* p. 178.
31. Michael Brecher, *op. cit.,* pp. 428.
32. See M.O. Mathai, *op. cit.,* p. 168-69.
33. S. Dutt, *op. cit.,* p. 87.
34. *Ibid.*
35. *Ibid.,* M.O. Mathai, *op. cit.,* p. 168.

36. S. Dutt, *op. cit.*, p. 88.
37. Indias Foreign Policy, pp. 377-78.
38. White paper No. I, Ministry of External Affairs, New Delhi, 1959, pp. 20-30, 39.
39. *Ibid.*, p. 49.
40. India's Foreign Policy, p. 377.
41. *Ibid.*, p. 108.
42. *Ibid.*, pp. 109, 119, 126.
43. *Ibid.*, p. 121.
44. For Nehru's views on the importance of geography and economic development for Indian Foreign Policy see India's Foreign Policy, pp. 22, 25, 32, 35, 41, 43, 47, 73, 83, 436.
45. *Ibid.*, p. 83.
46. *Ibid.*
47. *Ibid.*, pp. 68-69.
48. *Ibid.*, pp. 80-83.
49. M.S. Rajan, "India and World Politics in the Post-Nehru Era," International Journal, Winter 1968-69, p. 147.
50. See D.R. Mankekar, Lal Bahadur : A Political Biography, Popular Prakashan, Bombay, 1968, p. 67. For Lal Bahadur Shastri's biography see also B.S. Gujarati (ed.), A Study of Lal Bahadur Shastri, Sterling Publishers, New Delhi, 1965.
51. D.R. Mankekar, *op. cit.*, p. 117.
52. Broadcast to the nation over All India Radio on 116, 1964.
53. D.R. Mankekar, *op. cit.*, p. 117.
54. Broadcast to the nation over All India Radio on 117 1965.
55. D.R. Mankekar, *op. cit.*, pp. 146-147.
56. Published later on as Glimpses of World History, Lindsay Drummond, London, 1938.
57. Peter Lyon, "The Indian Bomb" : Nuclear Tests for "peaceful purposes"? The Round Table, London, October 1974.
58. Zahir Masani, Indira Gandhi : A Biography, Oxford University Press, Delhi, 1978, p. 238.
59. Zahir Masani *op. cit.*, p. 240.
60. K. Subrahmanyam, "Foreign Policy Planning", Foreign Affairs Reports, New Delhi, January 1975.

61. *Ibid.*
62. Mahendra Kumar, Theoretical Aspects of International Politics, Agra, p. 432.
63. M. Zuberi, Co-operative Denuclearisation, NPT Safeguards and India's Strategy in International Studies, J.N.U. April-June, 1993.
64. *Ibid., op. cit.*
65. Jasjit Singh, A Flawed Treaty in Savita Pande (ed), India and the Nuclear Test Ban, IDSA, p. 17.
66. Jasjit Singh, *op. cit.*, p. 18.
67. V.P. Datt, India's Foreign Policy, Vikas, New Delhi, p. 501.
68. V.P. Datt, *op. cit.*, p. 512.
69. V.P. Datt, *op. cit.*, p. 550.
70. Mahendra Kumar, *op. cit.*, p. 445.
71. *Ibid., op. cit.*, p. 450.
72. *Ibid., op. cit.*, p. 456.
73. Jasjit Singh, Extinguishing the Agni, India Express, 12 December, 1996.
73. *Ibid.*
74. The Times of India, 14 December, 1996.
75. Jasjit Singh, A Flawed Treaty, *op. cit.*, p. 5.

4

Introduction : India and Her Neighbours

India's foreign policy makers have always given a high priority to building friendly relations with our immediate neighbours. Despite his global perception of India's foreign policy, Prime Minister Nehru always underlined the importance of friendly relations with neighbours. Highest priority to neighbouring countries was also accorded by Prime Minister Shastri, though he had to lead the country in conflict with Pakistan. After 1971, Mrs. Indira Gandhi boldly pursued the goal of friendly bilateral relations with the South Asian neighbours in the spirit of Shimla Agreement. But, she could not achieve much success. Soon after assuming office as Foreign Minister in 1977, Atal Behari Vajpayee said that it was his (and Janata Government's) primary concern to co-operate with and seek confidence to immediate neighbours of India. He said that while government was fully aware of its responsibility to defend India's borders, it also wanted to honour and respect all its neighbours and their sovereignty and integrity. Vajpayee said that he desired tension-free relations in South Asia. Prime Minister Desai also emphasised the need for friendly relations with the neighbours whom he described as 'younger brother'. Desai said that as 'elder brother' India would have to be liberal and caring. Janata Government insisted on 'genuine' and 'real' non-alignment. The Gujral Doctrine (1996) was in continuations with the policy of 'elder brothers.'[1]

Ex. Foreign Minister Vajpayee's visits to Pakistan and China prepared ground for improved relations. Pakistan ex. President Zia-ul-Haq said that he was deeply impressed by sincerity of efforts of Desai and Vajpayee to improve bilateral relations. These efforts were vigorously pursued by Mrs. Gandhi as well as Rajiv Gandhi. Rajiv became the first Prime Minister after Nehru to have visited China. He also made efforts to strengthen friendly bilateral relations with Nepal, Bangladesh and Sri Lanka. During the Prime Ministership of P.V. Narasimha Rao relations with neighbours, showed clear signs of improvement. Narasimha Rao Government achieved fair amount of success in maintaining cordial relations with Pakistan. Nepalese Prime Minister Koirala who visited India in 1991 assured Rao that Nepal no longer dependent on China to fulfil its security requirements. Nepal's Communist Prime Minister Manmohan Adhikary visited India twice within a span of six months in 1995. Rao Goverment permitted port facilities for Nepalese goods in Bombay and Kandla in addition to existing facility in Calcutta. Efforts were made to ensure that Nepal did not become hostile to India as it was during 1989-90. India has made several attempts to solve Indo-Bangladesh problems and to have friendly relations with Bangladesh.

1. Indo-Nepal Relations

Nepal is the only Hindu state in the World. It is a landlocked country, situated on the Southern slopes of Himalayas. It has Tibet in the north and India in the south. It has common frontiers both with India and China. Ever since China established its full sovereignty over Tibet, Nepal's position has become all the more important for India. Prof. V.P. Dutt is of the opinion that 'India and Nepal are bound together by history, geography, kinship, religion, faith, cultural legacy and linguistic affinity. The two countries have shared their mythology of the Himalayas and their reverence for those tall and forbidding mountains.[2]

Nepal was not organised as a sovereign state till 1769 when Maharaj Prithvi Narain Shah brought about political unification of Nepal and established a monarchy. Another significant development took place in 1846 when Rana Jang Bahadur seized power and forced the king to become a nominal head of state. The Ranas became, and remained virtual rulers of Nepal till early 1951.

A conflict took place between Nepal and East India Company. In the process of British imperialist expansion, Nepal was defeated and forced to sign a treaty in 1816. The treaty provided for transfer of part of Nepalese territory to East India Company. A British Resident was posted in Nepalese capital Kathmandu and the country came under British influence. The British rulers of India had treated Tibet as a buffer between China and India, but situation changed after India's independence. Prime Minister Nehru said in the Lok Sabha on December 6, 1950 : "Apart from our sympathetic interest in Nepal, we are also interested in the security of our own country".

India's interest in Nepal was natural for historical, religious and strategic reasons. Recruitment of Gorkha soldiers in Nepal for British army continued even in 1947. Communist victory in China in 1949 made it apparent that it would establish its control over Tibet, and that would bring China in close ontact with the borders of Nepal. In view of communist power emerging in China it was natural for the United States to take interest in Nepal. India's security was perceived to be closely related to Nepal in the north. Meanwhile, there was a move in Nepal to draft a Constitution for the Himalayan Kingdom.[3] On Nepal's request, India sent Mr. Prakasa to assist the kingdom in drafting a constitution. Since the constitution then drafted went against the power of Rana's it was not enforced. The Nepali Congress was carrying on a movement for democratisation of the country's polity. Indian National Congress was always sympathetic to the movement for democracy in Nepal. A treaty of friendship negotiated in 1949 could not be signed as Nepalese Rana leaders resented India's proposal for a democratic structure of Government of Nepal.

Treaty of Peace and Friendship, 1950

India was keen to redefine Indo-Nepalese relations on the basis of sovereign equality and good neighbourly relations between the two. After about nine months of diplomatic activity and negotiations, a Treaty of Peace and Friendship was finally concluded between India and Nepal on July 31, 1950. It was clearly provided in the Treaty that, "neither government shall tolerate any threat to the security of the other by a foreign aggressor," and the two promised to "consult each other and device effective counter measures." In case of any threat from a third party or country. Nepal would ordinarily purchase war equipment from India. The Treaty provided that Nepal would consult India before buying war material from any other country. After such consultation Nepal would "import from or through the territory of India, arms, ammunitions, or warlike material and equipment necessary for the security of Nepal." Indo-Nepalese relations have been based on this treaty.[4]

After the signing of the treaty, India established 17th checkposts to watch the passes betwen Tibet and Nepal and Bhutan. These posts were jointly manned by Indian and Nepalese personnel. An Indian military mission was also established in Kathmandu for the organisation and training of Nepalese army.

The special relationship between India and Nepal was further underlined by the conclusion of a Treaty of Trade and Commerce, signed on the same day, *i.e.*, July 31, 1950. India agreed to make available to Nepal, to the maximum extent possible, commodities essential to its economy, also secure their routes and methods of transportation which were the most convenient and economical. The arrangement were reciprocal, but India was keen to help to develop the economy of Nepal. As Nepal is a landlocked country, the treaty of trade and commerce acknowledged Nepal's "full and unrestricted right of commercial transit of all goods and manufactures through the territory and parts of India." There were two other important provisions.[5] The treaty provided for fixing the same level of import duties on items imported from third countries. Nepal also agreed to levy on ground produce in that country, for export to India, export duties at rates that would enable Nepalese goods to be sold in India at prices not lower than the prices on which goods produced in India were sold. Thus, began an era of extensive economic co-operation and of economic assistance by India to Nepal. Nehru was keen that Nepal must enjoy all the attributes of independence and sovereignty. Even during democratic movement against the autocratic regime of Ranas, India adopted the attitude of restraint and patience.

Political Changes in Nepal

India played a significant role in the change of Nepalese political structure. The people of Nepal, inspired by freedom struggles in neighbouring countries, launched a movement for removal of Rana regime. People wanted to free the king from the control of Ranas and set up a constitutional government. The king, Maharaja Tribhuvan Narain Shah was fully sympathetic with the aspirations of people. Palace intrigues had become order of the day as Rana Shamsher Jang Bahadur imposed restrictions on the monarch. The Ranas were contemplating assistance from western powers. Indias anxiety was natural.[6]

Forced by circumstances, king Tribhuvan left the palace along with 14 members of the royal family and took shelter in the Indian Embassy in Kathmandu, on November 6, 1950. The next day, Rana Shamsher made an unsuccessful attempt to get the king back. Prime Minister Rana Shamsher, in a vindictive mood, "deposed" the King and declared a child Jainendra as the new king of Nepal. Maharaja Tribhuvan then flew to India with members of his family. India thus, was forced into the process of political change in Nepal, although Nehru family remained committed to independence of that country and the principle of non-involvement in the internal affairs of other states. India tried to be discrete mediator between various groups. As a resource negotiations held in Delhi in February 1951 King Tribhuvan returned to Nepal as its monarch. It was decided in the tripartite negotiations (King, Rana and Nepal Congress) that a democratic system would soon be introduced.

The co-operation between Ranas and Nepal Congress could not last long. A revolt was organised under the leadership of Dr. K.I. Singh. India co-operated with Nepal in taking police action against K.I. Singh, who was detained. He fled from jail in 1952. By early 1952, most political parties in Nepal had adopted anti-India stance. King Tribhuvan died in March 1955. His son Mahendra became the new king who assumed all powers to himself. Mahendra was already deputising for his ailing father sometime. Meanwhile, in 1954 Nepal was admitted to the United Nations. India had fully supported Nepal's membership of the U.N.

Anti-India Stance of King Mahendra

King Mahendra did not have the same feelings for India as his father had, and "palace politics soon came to be dominated by elements and forces not too friendly to New Delhi." The King began moving away from India. The rise of Chinese power in Tibet largely changed the situation for India-Nepal relations. Most of the opponents of King Mahendra were put in Jail and the monarch instituted the Rashtriya Panchayat System.[7]

India was disturbed at the setback to democracy in neighbouring Nepal. Regrets were expressed in Indian media on Nepalese developments. Leaders and supporters of Nepali Congress, who stood for parliamentary democracy, fled to India to work for a democratic government in that country. These developments disturbed the king. Thus began difficult phase of Indo-Nepalese relations. While India supported democracy, it was not prepared to support insurgency from its territory. King Mahendra rapidly moved closer to China. This resulted in Nepal securing economic assistance from China, expansion of Sino-Nepalese economic co-operation, balance of relationship, and reduction in the dependence on India. The young king was trying to convey the impression that he was a Champion of Nepalese nationalism. He approved his supporters anti-India Campaign. At times India felt that he was playing China against India. Mahendra had come to believe that India was supporting the rebels. This was not correct.

The then Prime Minister of Nepal T.P. Acharya was clearly pro-Chinese. During his visit to India in 1956, he said that Nepal was willing to act as a bridge between China and India. The Chinese Prime Minister Chou En-lai returned Acharya's China visit of 1956, in January 1957. He told the Nepalese that both the Chinese and Nepalese belonged to the same blood. He perhaps was intending to align China with Nepal, Bhutan and Sikkim. As Acharya began to speak Chou's language in international relations Indo-Nepalese relations were strained. He also said that India, in its own interest, should support the cause of Nepalese nationalism. A Sino-Nepalese Treaty relating to Tibet signed in 1956 caused anxiety in India.[8] China also promised a Rupees 6 crore assistance to Nepal. India never had any evil designes on Nepal. President Rajendra Prasad, during his 1956 visit to Nepal, assured the people of that country that India had no intention of interfering in the internal affairs of Nepal nor did India claim any of the Nepalese territory. In 1957, Dr. K.I. Singh became Prime Minister of Nepal. Even after the fall of Koirala Government (1960), Indo-Nepalese relations remained strained till 1961.

After Koirala was sacked by King Mahendra many leaders of Nepali Congress were arrested several of Congress leaders fled to India. The King blamed India for promoting anti-Nepal agitation, which further strained the relations.

Despite India's warning, King Mahendra entered into an agreement with China for the construction of Kathmandu-Lhasa Road. He praised the Communist Government during a visit to China. The Chinese aid to Nepal was highly appreciated in the press. The Chinese aid was described as liberal and selfless.

The 'Detente'

Nepal assumed greater importance in India's security perception after the Sino-Indian Border War of 1962. India's bid for improvement in relations was reciprocated. The soft-spoken Lal Bahadur Shastri, who was then Union Home Minister, visited Nepal and successfully removed doubts that the Nepalese had about India and its policy. Shastri laid the foundation of better bilateral relations. Nepal King's 13-day visit to India, and President Radhakrishnan's return visit, further cemented the improved relations. Appreciating the detente in Indo-Nepal relations the President of Rashtriya Panchayat, Surya Bahadur Thapa assured India that none would be allowed to attack India through its territory so long as even one Nepalese was alive.

Relations were further improved when Foreign Minister Swaran Singh visited Nepal in 1964 and signed an agreement of large economic assistance to Nepal. The King of Nepal again visited India in 1965 and conferred with Prime Minister Lal Bahadur Shastri. Nepal gave full support to India's position on Kashmir. The King appreciated the economic assistance being provided by India to his country.[9] However, the bilateral relations received another setback when a border dispute relating to Susta region arose. This region was claimed by Nepal in 1966. This one square-mile territory of Bihar-Nepal border remained a subject of dispute. Finally a boundary commission was appointed to resolve the same.

India's Economic Assistance to Nepal

Economic relations between India and Nepal were regulated by the treaty of trade and commerce of 1950. Nepal's main trading partner was India. By 1960, about 95 per cent o Nepal's trade was only with India. A programme of economic development of Nepal was undertaken by India. To begin with, India started construction of roads and transport system that would facilitate the movement of goods between the two countries, and within Nepal itself. As economic co-operation increased, many Indians acquired considerable economic stakes in Nepal. The Government of Nepal desired a greater access to foreign markets for the diversification of its international trade, which had to be routed through India. For India, large scale smuggling at the borders was causing anxiety. Negotiations for a new agreement resulted in the signing of an Agreement on Trade and Transit in 1961. It visualised setting up of a "common market" between the two countries. Goods originating in one country for sale in another country were generally exempted from any duties. Duty-free transit facilities were given by India to goods being exported to third countries steps against smuggling were to be taken by both the governments. Jute goods, match boxes and straw boards produced in Nepal were exempted from taxes by India. During 1962 Sino-Indian War, Nepal King tried to follow the policy of equidistance.[10]

Even after increase in Sino-Nepal trade, chunk of trade remained with India. In 1966-67, for example, the value of Nepal's exports to India was about 420,759,000 Nepalese rupees and of import from India about 465,113,000 rupees, during the same period exports to China were only to the tune of Nepalese Repees 5,562,000 and imports were worth 5,231,000 rupees. Nepal exported to the rest of the world goods worth about 60,941,000 rupees and its imports were of the value of Nepalese Rupees 10,921,000. Even in 1970-71, despite lapse of 1961 treaty and certain difficulties in economic relations, Nepal exported to India goods worth Nepalese Rs. 485,160,000 and imported items of the value of Rs. 783,050,000 while exports to China came down to 4,087,000 rupees and imports to Rs. 2,732,000 only.

In the field of economic assistance, by 1967 India had extended over Nepalese Rs. 50 crores for Nepal's economic development and had pledged another Rs. 40 crores, while China had advanced only Rs. 10 crores and pledged another about Rs. 35 crores. By 1967, India was the single largest aid giver to Nepal. Road building and power development were two major areas in which India assisted Nepal. India pledged to construct over 700 miles of roads in Nepal. Indian commitment included 78-mile Tribhuvan Rajpath (completed in 1956) which virtually became Nepal's life-line, the 128-mile long Sonalipokhara Highway and 40-mile East-West Highway. India also constructed a 46-mile road linking Kathmandu with Trisuli and a road in the Kosi project area.

India pledged to complete the Kosi project. In 1965, Prime Minister Lal Bahadur Shastri inaugurated work on Western canal of the Kosi project. The project was aimed at protection of Neplese areas from floods and to assure supply of electricity and water for irrigation. Despite a set back in 1966 on the border issue, India promised continued assistance for Nepal's development during Deputy Prime Minister Morarji Desai's visit in 1967. By 1968, Nepal was receiving about 40,000 kW of power generated by India, including supply from Kosi and Gandak power stations."[11]

India helped Nepal in the construction of the kingdom's first airport at Kathmandu. Besides, India also built three all-weather airports at Bhairava, Janakur and Biratnagar, and a fine weather airport at Simra. But, by this time China became an important factor in Nepal's economic as well as political relations. King Mahendra reaffirmed Nepal's decision to stay neutral between India and China. He added that Nepal's economic problems were normal problems of a land locked country, and he expected to receive all facilities allowed by international law. In late 1960's Nepal wanted to erode special relations with India, and secure free and uninterrupted transit facilities for trade with third countries including Pakistan. For India, China factor in Nepal's foreign policy had opened a dangerous situation. Goods were smuggled from India and then exported to foreign countries using the facility of duty-free trade. Foreign goods imported by Nepal under duty-free arrangement through India, also found their way into India and were sold at higher prices. India was not willing to allow duty-free trade with Pakistan.[12]

Demand for Withdrawal of Indian Personnel

Meanwhile, anti-India demonstrations were repeatedly held in Nepal. High level efforts were reported to have been made to spread anti-India sentiment and "turn the edge of Nepalese nationalism against India." Shortly after Foreign Minister Dinesh Singh's goodwill visit to Nepal in June 1969, Nepal made public demands for the withdrawal of Indian group in Kathmandu. Indians were based in these two positions in accordance with treaty agreements between the two countries. The demand for withdrawal was, thus, contrary to the treaty arrangement. Nepal was by this demand, questioning the very basis of Indo-Nepalese relationship. The demand was formally conveyed by Nepalese Ambassador in New Delhi.

India made it abundantly clear to Nepal that Indo-Sikkimese relations were exclusive concern of the two, and no third party or country had any business to express any concern. Nepal Prime Mininster N.P. Rijal's visit to India and discussions with our leaders led to immediate reduction in tension, and anti-India campaign faded out. Various steps were taken by India to normalise relations with Nepal. For example, in early 1976, India lifted all restrictions on the export of 44 items, imposed earlier which could now be brought freely in Indian market by Nepalese traders. Nepal was also assured by Foreign Minister Y.B. Chavan that Indian economic assistance would continue and that India would remain Nepal's major development partner.

Ever since King Birendra became the monarch, Indo-Nepal relations have remained generally cordial, though occassional irritants did appear. India participated in Nepal's development of power and irrigation projects. There were Indian aid and co-operation activities in areas such as road building, airport, construction, telecommunication, horticulture, agriculture, forestry, education and health.[13]

Bilateral Relations Since 1977

Indian National Congress which had been in power at the centre since 1947 was not only defeated and voted out of power, but even Prime Minister Indira Gandhi lost her seat in the Lok Sabha elections held in early 1977. The Janata Party Government that took over under the Prime Ministership of Morarji Desai pledged to give highest priority to friendly relations with India's neighbours. Foreign Minister Vajpayee reiterated India's resolve to improve relations with neighbours and forget the misunderstanding and tensions of the past. Without sacrificing India's national interests, Janata Government sought to undertake confidence building measures with the neighbours.[14]

The Desai Government tried to strengthen the cultural ties between India and Nepal. Prime Minister Desai's visit to Nepal opened the path for finding solution of the pending problems. Two trade agreements were concluded at the end of the visit. Nepalese Prime Minister Bista acknowledged in April 1978 that Indo-Nepalese relations had never been as cordial as they were at that time. India made no comments and took no action when movement for democracy began in Nepal. This was done to underline India's resolve not to interfere in the internal affairs of neighbouring countries.

The friendly relations with Nepal were further consolidated after Mrs. Gandhi returned to power in 1980. King Birendra visited India in 1981 and the visit was returned by President Sanjiva Reddy the same year. The King pressed for the acceptance of Nepal as the 'zone of peace' but India stood for the entire sub-continent or entire

South Asia, as zone of peace. Being a big power, and a neighbour of Nepal, China had been taking keen interest in Nepal. China had been trying to widen the rift between India and Nepal whenever tension developed in the bilateral relations. However, India continued to be Nepal's main trading partner. During 1984-85. Nepal's 52 per cent of total export-import trade was with India. Most of the goods produced in India and needed by Nepal are usually made available without much difficulty.[15]

India and Nepal became founder-members of South Asian Association of Regional Co-operation (SAARC), set up in 1985. This further strengthened the bilateral trade and commerce. The decision to establish SAPTA to enable preferential trading within 7 nation SAARC has been welcomed in both the countries. By 1996 all members of SAARC had submitted lists of goods to be treated on preferantial terms within South Asia and it was decided in 1997 that SAPTA would be replaced by SAFTA by 2001 AP to ensure for trading in the region.

When the Treaty of Trade and Transit expired in 1989 the Indo-Nepalese relations were once again strained. At that time Nepali Congress was engaged in struggle for multi-party democracy in Nepal. The king suspected that the Nepali Congress had the support of a good section of Indian people. The situation changed after the success of movement for democracy in April 1990.

Multi-Party Democracy and India-Nepal Relations

The age-old system of absolute monarchy in Nepal was replaced by constitutional monarchy in 1990. King Birendra agreed to the demands of the people for putting an end to partyless Panchayat System. Eventually, partyless democracy was replaced by party-based parliamentary democracy. Soon after assuming office as Prime Minister of India in December 1989, V.P. Singh expressed a desire to work sincerely for better Indo-Nepal relations. The process of normalised friendly relations was accelerated when Prime

Minister of Nepal came to India in June 1990. Two new agreements were concluded and signed by the two Prime Ministers on June 10, 1990.[16]

Economic relations between the two countries improved on account of liberalisation of their economies since 1991. The treaties of Trade and Transit of 1991, and their amendments in 1993 have also had positive results. During 1992-94 period, Indias commitment to Nepal's economic development continued to be expressed through various programmes. This included upgradation of the Jayanagar railway through the supply of new locomotives and carriages as also the supply of city sanitation equipment to Kathmandu Municipality. Boundary pillars in demarcated stretch of Indo-Nepalese border were repaired and steps were taken to extend co-operation in the field of ecological, soil conservation and other cross border problems.[17]

India's hand of friendship remains extended to Nepal.

2. Indo-Afghan Relations

Afghanistan is situated in Asia and is bounded on the north by Russian Turkistan, on the west by Iran and on the South by Pakistan. At its eastern borders there is China's Sinkiang province and it has a southern frontage of about 40 miles on Jammu and Kashmir. Thus, Afghanistan has got a link with India. During the middle of the 18th century, it first became a separate and independent state. It has been called "The Great Divide" between central and southern Asia which has, in the past, played a most vital role in history. From the beginning of the 19th century the British attempted to extend their influence in Afghanistan.[18]

British missions were sent to Afghanistan but the Afghan question did not assume particular importance for England until Persia supported by Russia, threatened to attack Herat a "key to India." The moves and countermoves of Russia and Britain concerning Herat precipitated invasion of Afghanistan by the British in 1839 (First Afghan War, 1839-

1842). But in England every moment beyond the frontier and every half-caught rumour from Central Asia was interpreted as an indication of the policy of St. Petersburg. After numerous efforts to establish Afghanistan as a neutral zone between the two powers the Clarendon-Gortcheakow Agreement of 1872-1873 was signed and the Oxus river was recognised as the northern boundary of Afghanistan and she was beyond the field of Russian influences. The Second Afghan War (1878-81) ended when a treaty was signed and a resident was appointed in Kabul. During World Wars I and II, Afghanistan observed an attitude of benevolent enutrality.

During the twenties the 'Red Shirt' movement began among the pathans of the N.W. F.P. The leader of the movement Khan Abdul Ghaffar Khan the "Frontier Gandhi," is very sympathetically disposed towards the Indian National Congress. He succeded in establishing a Congress Ministry for a long time under the Government of India Act, 1935. Pakistan was not sympathetic to this movement and imprisoned the "Frontier Gandhi."

The attitude of Pakistan against (Pakhtoonistan) has poisond Pakistan's relations with Afghanistan since 1947 and has, at times, created lot of foreign trade difficulties for the latter. Afghanistan opposes Pakistan's claim to sovereignty over the frontier tribes. She argues that the racial and cultural affinities between Afghans and pathans give Afghanistan special rights in the area. Attempts have been made by the U.S.A., U.K. and Iran to persuade the two countries to come to terms, but no arrangements have yet been made and the friction is increasing Afghanistan is a land without rail transportation. Only three main overland transit routes exist, through Iran, the U.S.S.R. and Pakistan. The route through Iran is long and expensive.[19]

Because of the dispute Pakistan has created difficulties in importing or exporting goods, money and men by Afghanistan. It threatened Afghan foreign trade seriously in 1950, 1955 and again in 1961. During March 1949, the

Afghan Government demanded the right of self-determination for the tribal people of the areas between the "Durand Line and the India." On June 12, 1949 a Pakistani plain dropped bombs in Afghan territory. The Afghans approached Great Britain for mediation but in vain."

Indo-Afghan relations are centuries old. A considerable part of present Afghanistan was under Indian empire during the days of Chandragupta Maurya, Ashoka and Akbar. As Dr. Radhakristan remarked. "Our relations with Afghanistan have close and intimate for centures. There was a time when India and Afghanistan formed parts of the same cultural region. For a while India and Greek sculpture fused in ancient Gandhra, the modern Kandhar. Even today we find in Afghanistan many relics of Indian culture and influence. It is essential for India's strategic security that the tribes men should be contented partners amongst the communites of the Indian Union."

On June 4, 1950, a treaty of peace and friendship between India and Afghanistan was signed in New Delhi by Pandit Jawaharlal Nehru and Afghan Ambassador, Sardar Najibullah Khan. It provides for intensification of trade relations between the two countries, the strengthening cultural contacts and mutual assistance.

After signing this treaty Pandit Nehru said in the Parliament, "Among our neighbours, there is Afghanistan with whom we have recently concluded a treaty of friendhsip. The history of our relationship shows conflicts as well as long periods of our friendship and cultural contacts. These old contact have not only been renewed between independent India and Afghanistan but have actually progressed." The Hindustan Times expressed its views as follows :

> "The treaty truly reflects India's foreign policy. It sets a new pattern in neighbourly relationship by wording the operating articles in such a way as to indicate that what is aimed at is strengthening of the cardial relations existing between the peoples of these countries."[20]

Indo-Afghan Friendship Association has been set up in India with the Minister of Educational and Scientific Research as its Chairman. A similar association has been formed in Kabul. Some technical experts were sent to Afghanistan on request on in 1958. Dr. Rajendra Prasad, the then President of India said, "It is gratifying to see that there is much common in the approach of our two countries to the world affairs. Both Afghanistan and India are wedded to policy of peaceful co-existence and non-alignment with power blocs. It is our conviction that the development of every country's resources for the good of the humanity at large and the maintenance of amity and good will among nations claims a priority that must transcend ideological differences.

The Prime Minister of Afghanistan Sardar Mohammad Daud Khan arrived in New Delhi on a tour of the country. Speaking at the banquet both Pandit Nehru and Sardar Daud Khan referred to the "Long memory of the past contacts" and the present common policies of striving for peace and non-affiliation pacts and power bloc's which had brought the two countries close to each other."

In his speech Pandit Nehru said "When I saw the word "ARIANA" inscribed on your.... aircraft.... I was reminded of the long ages during which we were connected. It was inevitable that we should be so connected we were neighbours and geography is a powerful factor which cannot be ignored..... The partition of India separated our direct boundaries and direct contacts (and because of illegal occupation of Kashmir by Pakistan we have go no common boundary for the present). But that makes little difference to our age-long community of interest and our old friendship has survived. Both our countries decided that we should not become a part of the international conflicts, of what is known as the cold war of military alliances and blocs of the great countries. This basic identity of view between us brought us nearer to each other, whether in the UN or elsewhere. We have often seen eye to eye with each other.[21]

In reply the Afghan Prime Minister said, "India today enjoys in the world a worthy position as free, young and vigorous country and the existing harmony in the stand of India and Afghanistan in the sphere of international affairs is a factor in bringing us closer together." Sardar Daud Khan was given a civic reception in the Red Fort at which Pandit Nehru said that the people of India and Afghanistan represented two branches of the same tree. In the Joint Communique issued by the two Prime Ministers on February 7, 1959, they reaffirmed the common aims of their governments to strengthen the close and friendly relations already existing between the two countries.

Pandit Nehru went to Afghanistan at the invitation of the Afghan Government for a five day visit from 14th to 18th September 1959. In his welcome speech, Sardar Daud Khan said, "I am very happy to welcome on behalf of the government and people of Afghanistan a distinguished and outstanding personality like Nehru of a great country, India, our friend." In reply Pandit Nehru said that he was happy to be able to come to Afghanistan and added "We have been good friends and neighbours for so long both in the past and in the present". In a Joint Statement, Nehru and Daud said that they had agreed that the existing cordial relations between their two countries should be sustained and enlarged. Nehru said in a speech at Kabul "I feel I have not come to strange people but a people among whom I feel perfectly at home. India has followed a policy of non-alignment. That is the policy of Afghanistan also. That is an additional factor which brings us together."[22]

Thus, both India and Afghanistan, writes Prof. S.C. Bhowmick, whether in the United Nations or outside have always seen eye to eye with each other. Both have adhered to the principles of Bandung Conference and regard them as genuine factors in maintaining Afro-Asian unity and harmony. Both follow the path of neutrality and non-alignment in regard to their foreign policy both are keen to prompt their economic development and reconstruction as speedily as possible. The existing cordial relations between them are sustained and enlarged by increased cultural co-operation and trade.

3. Indo-Japan Relations

In the Indo-Japanese consultative conference which ended in New Delhi, in the first week of March, 1966, Mr. N. Ushiba, Deputy Vice-Minister for Foreign Affairs, and the leader of the Japanese delegation said on the question of non-proliferation of nuclear weapons, basically the views of India and Japan were similar Mr. C.S. Jha, Foreign Secretary and leader of the Indian delegation said "Our views on most matters were found to be similar and even where we think differently we found the differences were not great."

On February 18, 1966, Mr. Essusaburo Shina, the Japanese Foreign Minister, made a pronouncement much in line with the Indian stand at the Geneva Disarmament Conference. He said, "We cannot tolerate the attitude of the nuclear powers which are keeping their own nuclear stockpiles and make it sound like a favour that they will unilaterally refrain from attacking non-nuclear countries."

"Indo-Japanese community of interest is manifest. It is all to the good that Indian officials set down with their Japanese counter parts to grapple with the problems confronting their countries. The habit of consultation, when well-formed, leads to concert, and Indo-Japanese concert will be a factor for stability in Asia. Apart from the governmental levels, we should encourage greater intellectual exchanges between India and Japan."[23]

4. Indo-Great Britain Relations

India and Great Britain are quite friendly. The main bond of friendship between the two lies in the Commonwealth of

Nations. When China invaded India, Britain came to the rescue of India and also gave her a good deal of arms aid. The economic relations between the two are also quite thick. Professor Toynbee rightly observed in this regard.

"It is one of the vital interests of the western people that this partnership of ours (English people) with the people of India together Constitute one of the two Asian quarters of the human race, and only two years after Great Britain had made a move for the reconciliation of Asia with the West by completing a liquidation of the British rule in Ceylon, Pakistan and the Indian Union and Burma. The Chinese who constitute the second quarter of the two Asian quarters of human race, were won over from the camp to the Russians.[24] If after thus losing the friendship of the Chinese sub-continent, our western world were to lose friendship of the Indian sub-continent as well, the west would have lost to Russia most of the old world except for a paint of bridge heads in Western Europe and Africa, and this might well be a decisive event in the struggle for power between the "free world" and Communism. So, the Indian Union the successor state of the British Empire, which covers most of the Indian sub-continent, and the state in which Hindus are prominent occupies a commanding position in the divided world of today, in which the United States and her associates are competing for world power with the Soviet Union and her associates."

Indians are also quite considerate towards Britain. It should be quite evident the following lines of R.G. Casep :

> "What is attitude of the mind of India toward the great world outside her source? A great many Indians regard themselves as having three choices of friends for the future the British the Americans and the Russians. They affect not to like any of these choices very much. However, at their present stage of development, they cannot hope to stand alone in the world as it is, of the three, if they had to choose they would undoubtedly choose the British, as being the devil they know."[25]

5. Indo-American Relations

Introduction

Immediately after the termination of Second World War, two erstwhile allies turned foes and gave rise to an unprecedented peace-time tension, called the Cold War. These two former allies were the United States of America and the Soviet Union. While other big powers like Britain and France were fully exhausted and weakened at the end of the war, USA and USSR emerged so powerful that they came to acquire the status of Super Powers. Both of them developed a bloc of nations each and the world, thus, became bipolar. By 1949, both of them had acquired nuclear weapons. Almost at the same time when the cold war was gaining momentum, India became free of British imperialism and emerged as a new democratic nation on the political map of the world. India took an instant decision to follow independent foreign policy without aligning itself with any of the two power blocs, in the context of cold war. India's policy of non-alignment is based on this basic decision. Thus, India decided to pursue the policy of freindship with all, but permanent alliances with none.[26]

In pursuance of this policy, it was natural that India not only maintained friendly relations with Britain, but also tried to develop cordial relations with both the super powers. India and the United States being the two largest democracies were expected to develop very close, friendly and co-operative relations. Generally, the two countries have maintained good relations between them, but there have also been periods of bitterness and virtual hostility. Such ups and downs are natural in the bilateral relations of any two large and self-respecting nations.

For almost five decades, the United States generally did not place Indo-US relations at the level of high priority. The US policy was altered in India's favour during the period of Chinese aggression on India in 1962. For sometime, Kennedy Administration adopted pro-India posture. But, the United States always gave primary attention to its own national interests and did not treat India as an equal nation. This country was generally given low priority by the US foreign policy makers. The United States found it difficult to appreciate India's approach to international politics, and often dubbed its non-alignment as pro-Soviet policy. As Prof. Stanlay rightly said American Relations have been "described as relations of unfriendly friends."[27]

Similarities and Irritants

India and the United States of America are the two largest democracies in the world. Despite differences in the size of their territories and population, the two countries have much in common. Their similarities can be easily traced into their colonial past. Both were ruled by Britain, though at different times. The 13 original states of the US were British colonies when they declared their independence on July 4, 1776. They later on won their struggle against British efforts to keep the colonies, and set up the United States in accordance with the constitution that they drafted in 1987 and ratified in 1789.

India had a long history and ancient civilisation when the British first arrived in the 17th century as traders and later established their empire. India waged a struggle for its independence against British colonialism and became a sovereign state in 1947. Indias Constitution, enacted in 1949 and enforced in 1950, has many similarities with the US constitution. Both countries are republics, governed by democratically elected representatives of people. Both India and the United States allow freedom to their people to elect their rulers in a free system of universal adult franchise. India, like the United States, has an administration responsive to the aspirations of people. It is not merely the similarity of polity and electroal systems, but there are basic features which are common in both the societies. India and the United States, both are plural societies where dissent is not crushed. People express their views freely and have full freedom of belief and worship. These freedoms are assured by the US Constitution (Amendment number one) and part III of the Constitution of India. Freedom of expression and freedom of the press are essential common features of two democracies. Not only governments are often changed in the two countries by their peoples, if they do not fulfil people's wishes, through democratic process, but also redressal of grievances is given primary attention. In India people do not hesitate to defeat Indira Gandhi in 1977, just as the Americans turned out Bush in 1992, even though he had inflicted a crushing defeat on Iraq.[28]

America is a country of migrants. India is not. Nevertheless in both the democracies people belonging to different races and having faith in different religions, live side by side and help the nation-building process. Secularism is an important faith in both the countries. Similarly, free market economy has now become a common feature, though before liberalisation in 1991 there was greater state control over economy in India than the US but both countries have always rejected the concept of "Command economies" which was so common in communist, and even Fascist, countries. A large presence of Indian migrants in the US, has also helped the communality of interest of the two countries.

India and the United States have had trade relations for over two hundred years. Indo-American trade had started in the 18th century when the Yankee Clipper ships brought ice from Boston and reached Calcutta, and returned to America carrying spices and textiles from India. Limited diplomatic relations were established in 1790 when US President George Washington appointed a consul at Calcutta. India's freedom fighters received friendly help and encouragement from the US people, from time to time. Inter-governmental exchanges tourism and religious experiences promoted friendly relations between the two countries.[29]

Two basic facts of international relations remain at the core of Indo-US Relations. First, relations among nations are always in conflict. Here we must distinguish between conflict and dispute. While conflict is a situation of disagreement which is unavoidable not only between nations and even between any two individuals. There can be no politics in a situation of total agreement nor in complete disagreement. Thus, conflicts consists of disagreement which will not lead to rupture. Dispute is specific expression of sharp differences on a given issue. It may be resolved peacefully, or result in rupture, even war.[30] The second constant feature of international relations is change. Relations between nations do undergo changes, for change is the essence of life. Both these phenomena have influenced Indo-American relations during last 50 years. There have been disputes, as in regard to approach of two countries on the question of crisis in Bangladesh (1971) and the issue of signing of NPT (since 1968) and CTBT, for few years, culminating in India's refusal to sign CTBT in 1996. The situation of conflict is natural whether on the question of non-alignment of military alliances like SEATO, or the question of Israel versus Palestine, or even the question of Soviet intervention in Afghanistan (1979-80)

There have been clear changes in perspective of two countries. For example, in early Nehru era, the US was not very appreciative of non-aligned policy of India nor did the USSR like it. Both blamed India to be in the other camp. But, when India responded favourably to UN Security Council resolution of June 27, 1950 on assisting South Korea, the Indian position was appreciated in Washington, but resented by the USSR. Later when India criticised American General, MacArthur's action threatening China (late 1950), the USSR suddenly became friendly and US became cool.

In 1962 when China attacked India the US offered help and support, but when Indo-Pak War of 1965 took place, the US took Pro-Pak stand. In 1971 (during and before) Indo-Pak war, US President Nixon openly came out in support of Pakistan and warned India of US intervention. US even sent its nuclear weapon-equipped 7th fleet into Bay of Bengal to terrorise India. Nixon want to the extent of asking China in 1971 to take steps in Himalayas to cause irritation to India. This Pro-Pak position was at its height in 1971.

Thus, main areas of irritation in Indo-US relation are the question of Kashmir, arms aid to Pakistan, generally pro-

Pak position of the US, India's non-alignment and since 1971 till 1991 India's very friendly relations with the USSR. The whole question of NPT and CTBT is still a major irritant. The consistent US support to Israel and India's recognition of PLO has been another irritant.[31]

After the end of Cold War, India and the United States have been actively looking for occasions and policies that can create more cordial and friendly relations between the two largest democracies. The termination of Cold War has freed Indo-US relations from the limitations of a bipolar world. However, their bilateral relations have been adversely affected on account of differences on the question of nuclear proliferation, missiles proliferation, regional stability, human rights and economic policies. According to American experts, the primary objective of the US policy in South Asia is to stop nuclear proliferation and the related regional tensions. The Clinton Administration of the US in 1992 took the initiative by advocating confidence building measures between India and Pakistan. President Clinton made it clear in 1997 that the US had no intention of mediating on the question of Kashmir between India and Pakistan. He told Pakistan Prime Minister that India and Pakistan must resolve their differences through direct bilateral negotiations.[32]

An important improvement in the Indo-US relations took place in the area of economic policies. The United States welcomed liberalisation of Indian economy and India's policy of inviting more and more foreign investment in industry, and development projects. An American delegation under the leadership of the then Commerce Secretary Ronald Brown, that visited India in January 1995, concluded several economic agreements in the areas of energy, industrial production, transport, petro-chemicals, financial services, telecommunication, and health care schemes. These agreements provided for massive US investment to the tune of 7 billion US dollars. American investment in Indian industry and commerce has grown rapidly. By 1997, even greater Indo-US economic co-operation was being projected.[33]

The US Agency for International Development was impressing upon the need to promote those development projects that were likely to bring about structural changes and help in the privatisation of Indian economy. These projects included greater participation of private sector in the production and development of energy, Joint Indo-American commercial and technological ventures, greater supply of water, better sanitation and provision for energy and better roads in urban areas, family planning and health care, food assistance and more efforts for women education. Both India and the United States signd in 1995, a common Agenda for the Environment, so that the two countries could jointly try to solve such common problems, affecting entire mankind, as the global warming ozone depletion and desertification. The other issues which were emphasised in the common Agenda were population explosion and investment in the field of human resources development.[34]

India and the United States both consider illegal traffic in drugs as a serious international problem. The two countries pledged to co-operate to tackle this problem at all levels. This joint programme can succeed by the exchange of anti-drugs intelligence information, and by effective control and check on production, trade and use of the harmful and injurious drugs.

India and the United States pledged to fight and abolish the curse of terrorism, and for this purpose decided to sign a comprehensive extradition treaty during the last decade of the twentieth century. This was an attempt at Indo-American co-operation in maintenance of law and order in the world.

India and the United States were engaged in co-operative action in several other areas in the end of the 20th century. Prominent among these areas were educational and cultural exchanges. Both the countries promised to make their cultural heritage available for the benefit of each other.

During the brief 18 months rule of Shastri, relations between India and the United States received clear set-back.

Sardar Swaran Singh, as Shastri's Foreign Minister played an important role in world politics. During this period, the US had started heavy bombardment on North Vietnam. India was critical of this action of the US, which resulted in strong anti-India opinion in America. One consequence of India's views on Vietnam was that Prime Minister Shastri's scheduled visit to the United States, in May 1965, was postponed by President Johnson on account of his "busy schedule" at home. This postponement was very humiliating for India. It was essential for India to give a suitable reply to the US President for this insult of a sovereign country.[35]

India-Pakistan War, 1965

India's humiliation by China in 1962 war had convinced Pakistan that India's defences were so weak that she could also easily defeat India, and capture the state of Jammu and Kashmir. Thus, Pakistan precipitated conflict with India first in the Rann of Kutch, and later in the state of Kashmir. Thus, in the wake of border war with China, came the war with Pakistan in September 1965. The use of American arms by Pakistan during Indo-Pak war of 1965 embittered Indo-US relations. India protested to the American Government that its arms were being used against India despite assurances of the US Government, that they would not be used against India, and asked America to prevent this. However, American leaders took no action in this regard and continued to maintain a pro-Pakistan stand. During that period six US ships were approaching India with certain supplies. When these ships were only 15 kilometers away from Indian coast, the US Administration asked them to return home. The United States, in accordance with its policy of equating India and Pakistan, suspended the economic assistance and military supplies (already in pipeline) to both the countries. India at that time had acute shortage of wheat and other food items. Thus, suspension of supplies of these essential goods to India caused serious hardships.[36]

However, US maintained neutrality in this war and refused Pakistan President Ayub Khan's request for active intervention. Washington also privately warned China against intervention in the Indo-Pak war, or otherwise, USA would provide military aid to India. This action of the US was much appreciated. These conflicts, followed by serious economic crisis, inflation and sharply dwindling foreign exchange reserves kept India's dependence on the US at a fairly large level. As Prof. V.P. Dutt put it, the thinning "bread basket" and the lenthening "hunger line" required substantial food imports from the country.[37]

Indira Gandhi and Indo-US Relations

The Tashkent Agreement signed in January 1966 by Prime Minister Lal Bahadur Shastri and Pakistan President Ayub Khan to normalise Indo-Pak relations. Within few hours of the signing of this agreement Shastri died at Tashkent. He was succeeded by Mrs. Indira Gandhi.

When Mrs. Indira Gandhi became the Prime Minister in January 1966, her first foreign policy move was to visit the US in March 1966. She was received warmly by President Johnson, who put pressure on India in regard to this country's relations with the Soviet Union. Mrs. Gandhi welcomed foreign investments. She drew attention towards China's aggressive policies. Relations with Pakistan were also discussed. India moderated its stand on Vietnam. Mrs. Gandhi emphasised the need for a political solution and the helpful contribution that a cessation of US bombing of North Vietnam would make in the search of political solution. Mrs. Gandhiji's visit in 1966 was perhaps the most serious, the most extensive and the most determined bid to establish and promote a close state of Indo-US relations.

India devalued its currency (rupee) apparently under the US pressure to India that was suspended by the US during 1965 Indo-Pak war, was not resumed though it was much less than the original assistance. Early Indira Gandhi period was marked by a major effort at aligning Indian and US policies as closely together as possible. The first formal bilateral talks were held in 1968. The Cold War ended (1989) and the Soviet Union actually disintegrated (1991) India has considerably improved its relations with the USA. It was felt that India has turned over-optimistic about the future of Indo-US relationship. As Malhotra opine "Thanks to initiatives taken by Rajiv Gandhi and Ronald Reagan, military co-operation on a limited scale between the two countries had begun. During Gulf-War (1991) the American war planes flying from South East Asia to Gulf destinations were allowed to be refuelled in India for which US was very appreciative, though Prime Minister Chandra Shekhar was criticised in many quarters for the facility provided to the United States.[38]

Until 1996 when under the Gujral Doctrine, relations were sought to be improved to India with all its neighbours, India viewed both Pakistan and China as a threat to its security. The intensity of this perception, has however, varied from time to time. But India has never regarded the United States as a power posing direct threat to its security. India has always regarded that the threat from the United States is indirect through its military alliance with Pakistan. For a long time since 1960s India had depended on the Soviet Union for its defence requirements. The United States saw India's special relations with the Soviet Union in the context of the cold war as strengthening Soviet position in South Asia.

The Problem of Nuclear Non-Proliferation

India's decision not to suspend, or terminate, its nuclear programmes, has been a major irritant in the Indo-American relations. India is committed completely for nuclear armaments. But India's views are not taken seriously by the United States. India has not conducted any nuclear test since 1974. The United States had always wanted that both India and Pakistan should sign Nuclear. Non-proliferation Treaty (NPT). India consistently refused to sign the NPT, because it regarded it as discriminatory. The USA went on putting pressure on India not only to sign NPT but also not to develop its missiles provoked serious criticism in America and elsewhere. India made no compromise on its stand on the question of signing NPT and later on the proposed Comprehensive Ban Treaty (CBT). India succeeded in blocking the CTBT in the Conference on Disarmament at Geneva in 1966 and voted against it even in the UN General Assembly. Thus, by 1997 Indo-US differences persisted on the question of NPT, CTBT, the missiles programme as also the whole issue of Kashmir and Human Rights.[39]

The Question of Human Rights

There has been a serious differences between India and America on the question of human rights also. The organisations like Ammesty International and Asia Watch, focussed attention on violation of human rights by India's security forces. Not only these organisations have demanded repeal of laws like TADA, passed by Indian Parliament. India did not permit representative of Ammesty International for nearly 14 years to investigate cases of alleged violations of human rights. Meanwhile, under the pressure of public opinion both inside and outside the country, a National Human Rights Commission was set up in India. This commission functions under the chairmanship of a retired Judge of the Supreme Court, and examines the allegations of violations to human rights. Even then, the United States always appears to be bothered about human rights in India.[40]

Economic Liberalisation in India and the USA

The United States have been very appreciative of the economic liberalisation programme initiated in 1985, but vigorously pursued since 1991 by te Government of P.V. Narasimha Rao. American government strongly supported India's case for financial assistance from the institutions like the World Bank and IMF. The second Clinton Administration asserted that it would continue to work for better economic ties with India. It is generally believed that India urgently required US investments in this country rather than the US wanting to invest in India. But, trade relations are normally for the benefit of both the countries. Clinton Administration was of the opinion that India was one of the top ten emerging markets. Ms. Albright had said in 1997, the US was likely to encourage commerce with India and increased investments in this country. But in view of the large size and potentials of India, the US assistance was still far from adequate.[41]

Conclusion

India and the United States of America are of the two largest democracies. It is argued that India, the largest democracy, and America, the most powerful democracy should be natural friends, if not allies. But this is an idealistic assumption. Despite numerous diversities the United States and other Western countries have found "That India Works." Still "the cussedness has not gone." To some extent India is responsible for this situation. In 1997, that India had moved a small number of Prithvi missiles, near Pakistan border the United States warned that it would "react very negatively" if either India or Pakistan tried to deploy ballistic missiles along their borders. It is unfortunate that even after the end of Cold War the United States has its sympathies with Pakistan.

It is in this background that President Clinton met Prime Minister Mr. I.K. Gujral in September 1997 and also his Pakistan counterpart. For the first time US President made a welcome move, when he made it clear that the United States had no intention of mediating on the Kashmir issue. Clinton made it clear that if India and Pakistan could resolve their differences bilaterally that would be the most welcome development. At the end of 1997 there were clear signs of improvement in the Indo-US relations as both India and Pakistan were engaged in taking confidence-building measures.[42]

In June 1998, the Summit talks were held on signing CTBT between US President Clinton diplomat Strabe Talbott and Prime Minister Vajpayee's representative Jaswant Singh. India made it clear it would adhere to CTBT only if her security was ensured and steps initiated for total nuclear disarmament.

The relations between the world's two largest democracies suddenly improved during and after the Kargil crisis. India is grateful nation. It appreciated the rational and practical response of the United States to the Kargil Conflict and the role of President Clinton played in defusing tension.[43]

The meeting between India's Minister of External Affairs Mr. Jaswant Singh and Foreign Ministers of several countries on the sidelines of UN General Assembly Session in September 1999 shows greater appreciation of India's position on various issues related to security disarmament and arms control.

Another significant development in Indo-US ties has been America's acknowledgement that it favoured a "stable, secure, powerful and united India."

REFERENCES

1. V.P. Dutt, India's Foreign Policy, Vikas, New Delhi, p. 252.
2. *Ibid.*, p. 256.
3. *Ibid.*, p. 278.
4. *Ibid., op. cit.*, p. 300.
5. On the occasion of Prince Birendra's Marriage reception.
6. V.P. Dutt, *op. cit.*, p. 233.
7. Chandrika Gulati, Liberation to Fundamentalism, New Delhi, p. 102.
8. *Ibid.*, p. 174.
9. Ministry of External Affairs Report, 1995-96.
10. V.P. Dutt, *op. cit.*, p. 323.
11. Chandrika Gulati, *op. cit.*, p. 115.
12. *Ibid., op. cit.*, p. 120.
13. *Ibid., op. cit.*, p. 125.

14. *Ibid., op. cit.,* p. 130.
15. V.P. Dutt, *op. cit.,* p. 138.
16. *Ibid.,* p. 189.
17. Ministry of External Affairs Report, *op. cit.,* 1995-96.
18. Mahendra Kumar Theoretical Aspects of International Politics, Agra, p. 432.
19. M. Zuberi, Cooperative Denuclearisation, NPT Safeguards and India's strategy in International Studies, JNU, April-June, 1993.
20. Jasjit Singh, A Flawed Treaty in Savita Pande (ed.), India and the Nuclear Test Ban, IDSA, p. 17.
21. V.P. Dutt, India's Foreign Policy, Vikas, New Delhi p. 501.
22. *Ibid.,* p. 502.
23. Jasjit Singh, Extinguishing the Agni, Indian Express, 12 December, 1996.
24. The Times of India, 14 December, 1996.
25. Jasjit Singh, A Flawed Treaty, *op. ci.,* p. 5.
26. Mahendra Kumar, Theoretical Aspects of International Politics, Agra, p. 432.
27. *Ibid., op. cit.,* p. 435.
28. *Ibid., op. cit.,* p. 450.
29. M. S. Rajan Studies in India's Foreign Policy, New Delhi, p. 286.
30. M.S. Rajan, *op. cit.,* p. 290.
31. M.S. Rajan, *op. cit.,* p. 295.
32. K.P. Misra, The conceptual framework of Non-alignment in Misra and Narayan (ed) Non-Alignment in Contemporary International Relations, p. 197.
33. *Ibid.,* p. 198.
34. V.P. Dutt, India's Foreign Policy, Vikas, New Delhi, p. 4.
35. V.P. Dutt, *op. cit.,* p. 8.
36. Rajan, *op. cit.,* 287.
37. *Ibid.*
38. See V.N. Khanna, International Relations, Vikas New Delhi.
39. Satish Kumar, Towards Stronger and Democratic United Nations—India's Role in International Studies, April-June 1993, p. 174.
40. *Ibid., op. cit.,* p. 178.
41. *Ibid., op. cit.,* p. 180.
42. *Ibid., op. cit.,* p. 185.
43. *Ibid., op. cit.,* p. 200.

5

India's Relations with Neighbouring Countries

Indo-Soviet Relations

India's relations with Soviet Union also did not begin on a note of cordiality. India's decision to become member of the Commonwealth and her opposition of the communist revolution in Malaya caused much misunderstanding in the Soviet minds. These actions were seen by the Soviet leaders as a clear advancement towards the Anglo-American bLoC. These doubts were further strenghtened after Indias support to Greece and her stand on Korea. Though India had announced on a number of occasions that she would not join either of the two bLoC's and would follow a policy of non-alignment. The Soviet leaders interpreted India's non-alignment policy as a mechanism of pre-western policy.[1]

But very soon the misunderstanding between the two countries started clearing up and their relations started improving. This was made possible by the combination of a number of factors. First of all, in 1950 India immediately recognised the communist government of China, which removed the doubts in the Soviet minds that India was essentially an anti-communist country. The role played by both India inside and outside the United Nations, as a leader of the anti-colonial powers also left a favourable impression on the minds of the Soviet leaders. During the Korean conflict also India showed her independent position. As a result slowly the Soviet leaders started appreciating India's policy of non-alignment.[2]

But the real improvement in the relations of the two countries took place only after the death of Stalin. The new Soviet leaders (Bulganin and Khrushchev) started the policy of improving relations with other countries with this view in 1955, the two Soviet leaders paid a visit to India and were given a warm welcome. One of the major factors which brought Soviet Union close to India was Pakistan's membership of the military alliances, sponsored by the Western powers and India's refusal to do the same. India also remembered how Soviet Union had come to her rescue by applying veto to the Security Council resolutions on Kashmir on more than one occasion.

The year 1956 witnessed closer as well as cooler relations between India and Soviet Union. During the Suez crisis of 1956 the two countries fully co-operated in condemning the action of aggression by Egypt, France and Israel against Egypt. They supported the resolution calling for halt of aggression and restoration of peace in the region. India not only supported the UN resolution along with the Soviet Union, but also offered forces for the UN, emergency forces in Egypt for the preservation of peace along with the armistice lines. In short, the two powers took an identical stand on the Suez crisis and co-operated with each other. However, the year 1956 also witnessed another crisis which caused much misunderstanding between the Soviet Union and India *viz.* the question of Hungary. In October 1956 a nationalist rising took place in Hungary and the Soviet Union sent its forces to suppress the same. India supported the cause of Hungarian people for freedom and wanted the Soviet the Soviet forces to be withdrawn.[3] However, the Indian government did not support the UN General Assembly resolution condemning the Soviet Union. Explaining India's stand Prime Minister Nehru said, "we are concerned with an attack on freedom anywhere in the world. We are concerned with an attack on freedom anywhere in the world. We are concerned also with strong nations dominating by armed forces, weaker countries. From the very beginning we made it clear that, in our opinion the people of Hungary should be allowed to determine their future according to their own wishes and that foreign forces should be withdrawn."

The Indias stand on the Hungarian question certainly caused some rift between India and Soviet Union, but the same was filled up very quickly. Soviet Union not only agreed to provide assistance for the Third Five Year Plan, but also agreed to make available Soviet oil at cheaper rates. In the Security Council it again vetoed resolution on Kashmir and fully endorsed India's stand on Goa. The two countries concluded a cultural and technical aid agreement in February 1960 which provided for the exchange of scientists, educationists, artists, and professors. The two countries also agreed to encourage the translation of each others literature, exchange of books and periodicals of non-political nature, exchange of radio and television programmes etc.

During the Sino-Indian conflict of 1962, Soviet Union extended support to India and agreed to co-operate with her in the building of MIG Fighter Planes in India. This was rather surprising that Soviet Union should support India against a communist country. It is said that Soviet Union extended support to India in view of her ideological conflict with China.

In 1965, when the Indo-Pakistan war brokeout, Soviet Union tried to bring about a cease-fire and arranged a meeting between Prime Minister Lal Bahadur Shastri of India and President Ayub Khan of Pakistan with a view to findout a solution for the outstanding problems through negotiations. It was mainly due to the efforts of Soviet Union that the two leaders met at Tashkent and signed the historic Tashkent declaration in January 1966. The two leaders declared their solemn resolve to restore moral and peaceful relations between their countries and to promote understanding between their peoples. They also pledged not to resort to force for the settlement of their disputes. The two leaders also acknowledge with gratitude the friendly and noble part played by Soviet Union in arranging and making the Tashkent meeting a success.[4]

In the year after the Tashkent, Soviet Union tried to develop closer relations with Pakistan as well. She offered to supply arms to Pakistan, which was somewhat irritating to the Indian leaders. However, continued to profess friendship towards the Soviet Union.

But probably the most significant development in Indo-Soviet relations took place in 1971 when the two countries concluded. "Treaty of peace, friendship and co-operation". From the Indian point of view the conclusion of this treaty was most fortunate. This treaty was concluded at the time when Pakistan was displaying a belligerent attitude towards India and there was every possibility of a war breaking out between India and Pakistan. In terms of the treaty the two countries agreed to respect each others foreign policy and to work for peace in Asia as well as in the world. The leaders of the two countries were to maintain regular contacts and hold discussions on important international problems.[5] The two countries also agreed to co-operate with each other as well as other countries in resolving international issues such as stoppage of arms race and bringing about of disarmament of both nuclear and conventional weapons under the international control. They were also to work for the elimination of colonialism and racialism from the world.

Another significant feature of the peace treaty was that the two parties were not to conclude military alliances against each other and also not to permit the use of their territory to any other power against each other. In case either of the party was subjected to an attack or threat of attack, the two countries were to hold reciprocal consultations with a view of eliminate the danger and to take effective measures for enduring peace and security of their country. By virtue of these provisions India was assured of Soviet support in case of Sino-American intervantion in a conflict between India and Pakistan.

Commenting on the significance of the treaty Swaran Singh, the then Foreign Minister of India said "We are convinced that this treaty will serve a shining example of how relations between two friendly countries can be and should be adopted and developed and how they can serve not only the interests of two countries but be an important stabilising factor for strengthening peace and security in this region and throughout Asia and the West.

The conclusion of this treaty marked a change in the foreign policy of India. This was probably the first treaty concluded by India with any big power. The Ex. Prime Minister Mrs. Indira Gandhi said, Indo-Soviet treaty could act as a deterrent against any rash adventure on the part of Islamabad. She further asserted that under the treaty 'India was free to exercise such options as it wanted in the national interest without any restraint. India would never give up its right to decide and act independently, as this would mean surrendering national sovereignty.[6]

Thus, India's relations with the Soviet Union continued to grow along friendly lines and reached a saturation point in early seventies. However, after the defeat of the Congress Government and emergence of Janata party in 1977 to power, it was expected that the close relations between the two countries would suffer a set back. There was an open demand for the snapping of the Indo-Soviet treaty in certain quarters. The doubts were further strengthened by pronouncements of certain Janata party leaders. For example, Prime Minister, Mr. Morarji Desai told the critics of Indo-Soviet treaty that the treaty would not be permitted to stand in the way of friendly relations with other countries. The leaders of the two countries exchanged mutual visits and decided to continue friendly relations. In fact, they pledged to further improve their relations. In view of these assurances and pledges the Indo-Soviet treaty was permitted to continue unmodified.

Mrs. Gandhi's Second Tenure

The detente at the international level had reached a high water-mark with the signing of Helsinki Final Act in 1975. But the environment suddenly changed with the commencement of the New Cold War as a result of the Soviet intervention in Afghanistan in 1979. This intervention was denounced by the West as Soviet invasion of Afghanistan, but was described by the Soviet supporters as painful Soviet decision because of the United States and Pakistan were threatening the Soviet friendly Afghan regime. Further, after the fall of Janata Government, Mrs. Gandhi had come back to power in January 1980. The soft line adopted by Mrs. Gandhi was strongly criticised as compromise with the policy of non-alignment and clear shift towards the Soviet Union. During the Soviet President Brezhnev's visit to India in December, 1980, the Soviet military presence in Afghanistan was not even mentioned. However, Mrs. Gandhi and Brezhnev did express their concern over tension in South-West Asia. They reiterated their commitment to political solution of the problems respecting independence, sovereignty territorial integrity and of the problems respecting independence, sovereignty, territorial. Integrity and non-aligned status of countries of the West Asian region.

Bilateral Relations in the post-Brezhnev period. India was assured after the death of Brezhnev in 1983 that Indo-Soviet relations would continue to be cordial and friendly. Bilateral trade continued to grow. After Mrs. Gandhi's assassination in October, 1984, India's leadership went into the hands of her son Rajiv Gandhi. Indo-Soviet relations were further consolidated during the period that the two countries were led by Rajiv and Gorbachev. The two countries had more or less identical views on most of the international questions. Rajiv Gandhi asserted a number of times that the Soviet Union had stood by India in all difficult times. Therefore, Indo-Soviet friendship would be maintained at high level. Rajiv Gandhi went on a 6-day visit to the Soviet Union in May 1985. Both the countries signed agreements for economic and technical co-operation whereby Soviet assistance to India was considerably increased. A new Soviet credit of Rs. 1160 crores was announced. It was also agreed that the USSR would provide assistance for a thermal power project of 840 megawatt capacity, and certain other schemes.[7]

A significant Delhi declaration as issued at the end of Gorbachev's Delhi visit. It was signed by Rajiv Gandhi and Gorbachev. On his arrival in India Gorbachev had warned that if Indo-Pak disputes were not amicably solved then it could lead to serious consequences. He had expressed the hope that like India, Pakistan would also behave like a good neighbour. Another significant announcement was made by him. He said that the USSR would not attempt to improve relations even with China at the cost of Indo-Soviet friendship.

Ten-point Delhi Declaration was according to Rajiv and Gorbachev an effective step in the direction of comprehensive nuclear disarmament. In addition to the forceful Delhi Declaration, an economic protocol was also signed by India and the Soviet Union. Accordingly, the USSR agreed to give a long-term credit of Rs. 2883 crores on nominal interest for renewal of certain old projects and starting of some new projects. Cultural festivals were organised in the two countries since 1988 for better cultural exchanges. Several artists promoted the feeling of universiality and equality.[8]

The Indo-Soviet Treaty of peace, friendshp and co-operation was as mentioned earlier, renewed in 1991 for a further period of 20 years. This was a proof of sustained ties between the two countries and in a way, brought India under the Soviet nuclear umbrella. The Cold War had ended at the end of 1989, but a new environment had been created in the Soviet Union by various reforms initiated by party General Secretary Gorbachev. Meanwhile, in India power was transferred from Rajiv Gandhi led Congress

Government to a minority Janata Dal Government. After a brief period of lack of warmth, Prime Minister V.P. Singh paid a visit to the USSR in 1990. This renewed the warmth in the bilateral relations. The Soviet position on Kashmir was reiterated. It was decided the renew the 1971 Indo-Soviet Treaty, and it was decided to continue till 1995 the rupee rouble trade arrangement. Thus Indo-Soviet relations showed mature and stable friendship.[9]

During the period 1994-96, several high level visits were exchanged between the two countries. These included Narasimha Rao's visit to Russia in June-July 1994, when the two countries agreed to take necessary measures to remove the bottle necks in the bilateral trade. An Indo-Russian Summit was held in March 1997 when Prime Minister H.D. Devegowda visited Moscow and had extensive discussions with Boris Yelstein and Prime Minister Victor Chernomyrdin. The visit turned out to be a high water mark and several agreements were signed at the conclusion of these talks. These included the agreements for the avoidance of double taxation, co-operation and mutual assistance in customs, plant protection and a plant quarantine and the extradiction treaty. An agreement for mutual legal assistance in criminal matters, a consuler convention and an agreement for phical culture and sports were also signed. In addition to these agreements the Russians also agreed to assist India in expanding its nuclear capacities for peaceful purposes.

Indo-Russian relations continued to be strengthened by putin and Vajpayee governments. President Putin paid a highly successful visit to India in October 2000. The two countries chalked out steps to set their bilateral relationship on a new-footing. Besides strategic parternership and trade and cultural co-operation the two countries also pledged to fight international terrorism.

Indo-Bangladesh Relations

Bangladesh is the eight most populous country in the world. It has a total area of 1,39,523 sq. kilometres. The birth of Bangladesh in December 1971 was a direct outcome of the Indo-Pakistan war in which Pakistan troops surrendered unconditionally in erstwhile East Pakistan. It was culmination of revolt of Bangladeshis against tyrannical Pakistani regime. The revolt had begun in March 1971, when the most popular leader of Awami League Sheikh Rehman was arrested and taken to a West Pakistani Jail. India had full sympathy with the people of East Pakistan in their struggle for independence. The emergence of Bangladesh was described as an event of major importance in the sub-continent. All efforts by India and its Prime Minister Mrs. Indira Gandhi, to persuade Pakistan for the negotiated settlement with Awami leaders had failed. Pakistani President Yahya Khan was determined to seek a military solution to the crisis. He failed in this and had to handover power to Z.A. Bhutto after East Pakistan became independent Bangladesh.[10]

Soon after recognition of Bangladesh, while the war was still going on the first Indo-Bangladesh Treaty was concluded on December 10, 1971. The treaty, signed by Mrs. Gandhi and acting Bangla President Nazrul Islam, set-up a Joint India-Mukti Bahini command under an Indian general to liberate Bangladesh from Pakistan military rule or regime. The Indian army would leave Bangladesh as soon as normalcy was established in that country. India pledged to protect the territorial integrity of Bangladesh, and promised economic assistance for the reconstruction of the new state. Details about return of Bangladeshi refugees to their country were also worked out."

India pleaded with major powers to exercise their influence over Pakistan to secure the release of Sheikh Rehman who was under detention. The Sheikh was released on January 8, and he arrived to a tumultuous welcome in New Delhi on January 10, 1972. He profusely thanked India for the sacrifices made by this country for his country. After he assumed the office of Prime Minister of Bangladesh in

Dhaka, India invited him for an official visit. He visited Calcutta from 16-18 February, 1972 where he held foreign talks with Prime Minister Indira Gandhi. The two leaders resolved that Indo-Bangla relations would be guided by the principles of "democracy, socialism, secularism, non-alignment and opposition to racialism and colonialism in all its forms and manifestations.

India assured Bangladesh that it would never interfere in its internal affairs. India also announced that as agreed, its troops would be withdrawn by March 25, 1972. The two Prime Minister promised to ensure, as far as possible that trade between two countries can be regulated through official channel so that anti-social elements could not take advantage by smuggling.[12]

Indo-Bangladesh Treaty of Friendhsip and Peace

Sheikh Mujibs visit to Calcutta was returned by Mrs. Indira Gandhi's official tour of Bangladesh in March 1972. At the end of Indo-Bangla Summit talks the Treaty of Friendhsip and peace was signed on March 19, 1972. It was stated in the joint declaration that the treaty was concluded "to give concrete expression to the similarity of views, ideals and interests." It was inspired by the ideals of peace, secularism, democracy, socialism and nationalism. Mrs. Gandhi assured Bangladesh of India's full support and co-operation in securing its admission to the United Nations.[13]

The Treaty of Friendship and peace was signed for a period of 25 years. India withdrew its troops from Bangladesh even before signatures were put on the Treaty, though they could have stayed on till 25th of March. It was provided in the treaty that the two countries would not interfere in the internal affairs of the other and that they would respect the territorial integrity of each other. The preamble spoke of friendship between the two countries based on sacrifice by their peoples leading to emergence of

Bangladesh. The two countries promised to promote international peace and security and to fight against imperialism and racialism. The two countries would seek solution of international disputes through co-operation rather than conflict. It was also provided in the Treaty that in case of aggression, or threat of aggression, against either India or Bangladesh, the two countries would consult each other and try to find a solution to ensure security of both the High Contracting parties. The two countries would not attack each other, nor help any third country against the other signatory. None of the parties to this treaty would enter into an agreeent with a third country that might be against the interest of the other party. They would not enter into any military alliance aimed against the other. Both the parties expressed their faith in the principle of peaceful co-existence. The two countries agreed to co-operate with each other in economic, scientific and technological field. They would work together in areas such as irrigation and education, culture and sports. Thus, the Indo-Bangladesh Treaty of friendship and peace covered wide range of bilateral relations as also their commitment to international peace and security.[14]

The Trade Agreement

The signing of friendship treaty was followed by the conclusion of a comprehensive trade agreement on March 25, 1972. The short-term agreement provided for creation of a duty free zone upto 16 km. on both sides of Indo-Bangla border. People could cross the border once a day and carry not more than Rs. 100 with them to purchase their essential requirements of daily use. The second part of the agreement provided for rupee trade upto 50 crores in a year. This enabled Bangladesh to secure market for its products including fish, raw jute, hides and skins and newsprint. India on the other hand, could supply to meet Bangladeshi requirements of tobacco, cement, minerals, machinery etc. The third part of the treaty dealt with trading in foreign currencies (foreign exchange). The two countries could purchase from each other any goods to be sold against foreign exchange.[15]

The Treaty of Friendship and the Trade Agreement—were concluded in the spirit of equality and mutual benefit, friendship and good neighbourliness. Thus, during the first year after the emergence of independent Bangladesh there were signs of only friendship and co-operation between two countries.

India's Prime Minister had detailed consultations with Bangla Prime Minister Sheikh Mujibur Rehman before she went to attend Shimla Conference where an agreement was concluded with Z. A. Bhutto of Pakistan on various issues arising out of 1971 war. India made it clear to Pakistan that it was not ready for any solution regarding prisoners of war detained in India which was not acceptable to Bangladesh. Bangladesh was keen to try all these pows who had committed atrocities.

Bhutto was equally keen to get 90,000 prisoners of war (detained in India) repatriated in accordance with the agreement concluded in 1973. Pakistan refused to recognise Bangladesh till all pows were repatriated. China, who stood by Pakistan during and after the crisis, not only refused to recognise Bangladesh, but even exercised at its veto in the Security Council or Bangla application for membership of the UN in 1972.[16]

Pakistan recognised Bangladesh on February 22, 1974. She had earlier extended invitation to Bangladesh to attend the Islamic Summit at Lahore (1974). When Pakistan did recognise Bangladesh, it was said that it was to facilitate Pakistan-Bangladesh friendship and help pro-Islamic and pro-Pakistan elements in Bangladesh. Mujib attended the Islamic meet which gave Pakistan an opportunity to intensify anti-India and pro-Islamic campaign in

Bangladesh. Early in 1975 India and Bangladesh had signed an agreement on sharing of Ganga-waters. The upset Pakistan, and its government took steps to weaken Indian influence in Bangladesh. It talked of "India's new imperialist attitude" and Bangladesh's subservient position. Pakistan Prime Minister Z. A. Bhutto visited Bangladesh in June 1975. Not only the two countries agreed to establish diplomatic relations, but Bhutto also offered economic aid to Dhaka. The discord between India and Bangladesh was systematically created.

Assassination of Mujibur Rehman and Indo-Bangladesh Relations

A number of forces hostile to India were active in Bangladesh. It was generally believed that the government of Sheikh Mujibur Rehman was "faltering economically and wobbling administratively." Prices were continuously rising. Mujibur Rehman declared emergency on December 24, 1974 and assumed all the powers himself. He fariled to check corruption hoarding etc. He brushed aside the intelligence reports and refused to believe that his "children" could do any harm to him. Sheikh Mujibur Rehman, the creator of Bangladesh, the Bangabandhu was killed along with members of his family. Fundamentalism had emerged and secularism became a victim in the new military regime. The period after Mujib's assassination was quite disturbing for India. After Mujib's assassination power was assumed by Lt. Gen. Zia-Ur Rehman. The coup leaders made it clear that Bangladesh was no more secular, though Mujib's Bangladesh was secular, democratic, republic and there was no place for army in politics. Since 1975 Bangladesh come to be ruled by pro-Pakistani and anti-Indian forces.[17]

Bangladesh was ruled by Gen. Zia-Ur Rehman till may 1981 when he was killed . His successor civilian President, Sattar was overthrown in a bloodless coup on March 24, 1982 and Lt. General Ershad assumed power. Lt. General

Ershad took his country closer to Islamic oil producing countries. The attitude of new regime towards India was marked by confusion. The problems relating to Farakka barrage and sharing of Ganga waters were major issues of conflict between India and Bangladesh.

Sharing of Ganga Waters

The most difficult and nagging problem between India and Bangladesh retes to sharing of Ganga waters. The Ganga waters dispute between India and Bangladesh is mainly concerned with the sharing of waters during lean season. The crux of the problem is that if India withdraws 40,000 cusecs, Bangladesh receives only 15,000 cusecs which is highly insufficient to meet its needs. The extraction of this larger amount of water by India gives rise to multifarious problems in Bangladesh. Thus, the dispute between India and Bangladesh relates to equitable sharing of Ganga waters by the two countries.

The Ganga waters dispute between India and Bangladesh is mainly concerned with sharing of waters during lean season, January to May particularly mid-March to mid-May, when the flow of Ganga reduces to minimum level of 55000 cusecs. The crux of the problem is that if India withdraws 40,000 cusecs, Bangladesh receives only 15,000 cusecs which is highly insufficient to meet its needs. The extraction of this larger amount of water by India gives rise to multifarious problems in Bangladesh. Thus, the dispute between India and Bangladesh relates to equitable sharing of Ganga waters by the two countries.[18]

In 1972 a Joint Rivers Commission was set up accordance with Mujib-Indira agreement. It conducted detailed survey and identified weak point which could be strengthened and gaps that could be closed by further embankments. After Ambib's 1974 visit to India, an agreement was concluded on temporary basis for the alLoCation of Ganga waters. It was signed in 1975 and was called 'breakthrough.' India agreed to allow about 80% of water to Bangladesh in six weeks of lean period. This was a gesture of goodwill on the part of India. But, with the assassination of Mujibur Rehman in August 1975, Indias attitude became hard more so because anti-Indian forces had become active and vocal in Bangladesh.

The 1977 Agreement

The Government of Morarji Desai in India accorded a high priority to the improvement of relations with India's neighbours. After negotiations between the two countries, an agreement for five years, was concluded on sharing of Ganga waters in November 1977. It was a bilateral agreement signed at a time when Zia-Ur Rehman was working for stability of Bangladesh and regional co-operation in South Asia. 1977 agreement offered partial solution as it dealt with only the sharing of Ganga water during the lean period. Attempt was made to regulate flow of Ganga at Farakka during five month period, January to May each year. Sharing of water was to be regulated for every 10-day period. Thus, for example, from January 1 to 10, out of a total flow of 98,000 cusecs India would draw 40,000 cusecs and Bangladesh would share 58,000 cusecs. At the peak of lean period April 21 to 30, Indias share would be 20,500 cusecs and Bangladesh would get 34,500 cusecs. This was the best that India could offer to Bangladesh. Prime Minister Desai described this agreement as an achievement of Indian diplomacy.[19]

The agreement of 1977 expired on May 30, 1982. Fresh agreement had to be concluded. A meeting between Gen. H.M. Ershad, the then President of Bangladesh and Prime Minister Indira Gandhi opened new horizons in the bilateral relations. A fresh Memorandum of Understanding (MoU) was signed in 1982. The 1977 agreement was extended for 18 months. It was agreed in 1982 that if the actual availability of water during a 10-day period was higher or lower, then it would be shared in proportion applicable to that period. The agreement was renewed in 1983 and again in 1986. It finally lapsed in 1988 and India began releasing water on ad-hoc basis.

Other Bilateral Issues

Among other problems in India-Bangladesh relations is the problem of Chakma refugees who have mostly taken shelter in Indian state of Tripura. India is facing another problem concerning Bangladeshi nationals. A very large number of Bangladeshis, mostly belonging to economically weaker section, have been illegally entering India. It is difficult to distinguish between Indians belonging to West Bengal and Bangladeshi migrants. Some non-Muslims have been illegally coming as refugees because of occasional communal tensions. There are about 4 lakh such illegal migrants in Delhi alone. Their arrival without valid travel documents is made easy by the lack of any natural border between two countries. India's proposal to do fencing of the border with barbed wires was opposed by Bangladesh. India had made it clear to Bangladesh that it wanted barbed wires as preventive measure against illegal migration. It was not contrary to 1975 treaty of friendship.[20]

Indo-Bangladesh Joint Business Council has been exploring possibilities for expansion of economic and commercial co-operation and for setting up of industrial projects and joint ventures. Bilateral trade has been gradually increasing. Sheikh Hasina Wajed daughter of Bangabandhu Mujibur Rehman took over the Prime Minister in 1996. Hasina Government negotiated with India a treaty for sharing of Ganga waters for 30 years. The treaty was signed in New Delhi on December 12, 1996 by the two Prime Ministers, Mr. H.D. Deve Gowda and Sheikh Hasina Wajed. The treaty has a provision of mandatory review every five years. The review may take place even after the two years with the scope for adjustments, if required. The treaty may be renewed with mutual consent. Deve Gowda described the signing of the treaty as a "landmark event in Indo-Bangladesh relations." The 30-year treaty was described by Sheikh Hasina and Deve Gowda as "fair and just" to both the countries.

Indo-Pak Relations

The independent sovereign dominions were born in mid-August 1947. In a message on August 15, 1947, Jawaharlal Nehru had said : "I want to say to all nations, of the world, including our neighbour country, that we stand for peace and friendship with them." This has been the main thrust of India's foreign policy for 50 years. In fact, Pakistan's Governor General and creater M.A. Jinnah had also said that "we want to live peacefully and maintain cordial relations with our immediate neighbour and with the world at large." But, what actually happened between India and Pakistan was conflict", discord and even wars. The undeclared war took place an ugly turn when India and Pakistan fought a war in 1965. Once again in 1971, Pakistan forced a war on India and got defeated. Since 1971, there has been no armed conflict in the form of a war, but border clashes along the line of control in Jammu and Kashmir became a common feature. India consistently sought peaceful, cordial, and friendly relations with Pakistan, as with all other countries in the world.[21]

India's relations with Pakistan occupy a central position in her foreign policy, because her relations with other countries were largely influenced by the nature of its relations with Pakistan. The hostile relations between India and Pakistan were inevitable in view of the manner in which the state of Pakistan was created and the problems created by the partition which strained the relations between the two countries included the problem of refugees, evacuee property, minorities etc. But the factor which proved to be a major stumbling bLoCk in the way of developing cordial relations between the two countries was the feeling existing in Pakistan that India had not reconciled herself to the partition of the country and would make an attempt to destroy her entity at the first available opportunity. Though the problems of refugees evacuee property and minorities, were solved through mutual negotiation and agreements, yet certain other factors continue to strain the relations between the two countries in the subsequent years. These included the Kashmir problem the water dispute, Pakistan decision to join the western military alliances, transfer of Pakistan occupied Indian territory to China through an agreement etc. It shall be desirable to analyse the relations of the two countries in the light of these issues.[22]

1. The Kashmir Problem : The issue of Kashmir has proved to be a permanent thorn in the Indo-Pak relations. The state Jammu and Kashmir like other states of India was given the choice to join either India or Pakistan or retain independent status under the Indian Independence Act 1947. However, the king of Kashmir (Hari Singh) refused to accede to either of the countries and asked for a standstill agreement both with India and Pakistan pending a final decision regarding accession. Though no such agreement could be concluded with India Pakistan accepted the agreement. Simultaneously she also started applying economic pressure on the ruler to gain Kashmir's accession to Pakistan. But when the economic pressure proved ineffective, Pakistan encouraged the tribes men to invade Kashmir. These tribes were assisted by the regular troops of Pakistan army. As the king of Kashmir was not able to meet the threat of the raiders, he appealed to the Government of India for assistance. However, the Government of India refused to send troops unless the king signed letter of accession in favour of India. Ultimately the king signed the accession letters and the Indian troops were sent to Kashmir. Pakistan not only refused to recognise the accession of Kashmir to India, but also continued to assist the Azad Kashmir (An area of Kashmir forcibly occupied by Muslim tribesmen).

As the discussion failed to prove any agreed solution, India took the matter of Kashmir to Security Council under Article 35 of the UN Charter and charged Pakistan of an act of aggression against India. The Security Council after much consideration adopted a resolution calling on India and

Pakistan to withdraw their troops and tribesmen respectively. It also favoured the establishment of an interim government containing representatives of the major political groups. It also suggested that a five men UNICIP be sent to Kashmir to exercise their good offices in resorting peace and arranging a plebiscite.[23]

However, the resolution failed to satisfy both the countries. The UNICIP after working for about one month recommended a cease fire and subsequent negotiations of a Truce agreement on 13 August, 1948. The Commission submitted a plan for free and impartial plebiscite, after the peace had been resorted to the state. These proposal of the commission were accepted by Pakistan as well as India and the cease-fire agreement was signed. The agreement was come into force on 1 January, 1949. However, the implementation of the agreement could not be effected due to disarmament between the two parties on the demarcation of cease-fire line and the whole issue cameback to the Security Council.

Further, in February 1950, the Security Council appointed Sir Owen Dixon of Australia as a mediator. He came to the sub-continent in May 1950 and worked in India, Pakistan and Kashmir. Ultimately he proposed a plan which combined the twin principles of partition and plebiscite. However, his proposals were not accepted to either India or Pakistan. He admitted the failure of his mission tendered his resignation. He was followed by Dr. Frank P. Graham of USA who continued negotiations with the two governments from June 1951 to February 1953. However, the Graham mission failed.

In the meanwhile certain important developments had taken place in Kashmir. The popularly elected constituent Assembly confirmed its accession to India on 6 February 1954. On 19 November, 1956 the Assembly adopted a constitution by which the state was made an integral part of India. This accession was formalised by India on 26

January, 1957 and it was also made 'irrevocable' Pakistan was not happy with these developments and continued to insist on plebiscite at the United Nations. Thereafter, India took the stand that Kashmir's accession to India was "Full, complete and Final," and it would not be desirable to review the same. Pandit Nehru justified India's changed stand on Kashmir and said or asserted that India could not ignore the constitutional developments and economic progress in Kashmir. The holding of plebiscite would mean "uprooting of things that have become fixed—legally, constitutionally and practically."[24]

The issue of Kashmir once again shot into importance soon after the Kutch dispute in 1965. The Security Council authorised Uthant the Secretary-General to personally visit India and Pakistan and work for a peaceful settlement. Though the cease-fire was effected as a result of the efforts of the Secretary-General, but the negotiated settlement was made possible only through the efforts of Soviet Union. The Soviet Union took a lead in arranging a meeting between Prime Minister of Lal Bahadur Shastri of India and President Ayub Khan of Pakistan at Tashkent, and the meeting was held from January 3 to 10, 1966 to formalise peace between India and Pakistan. The Tashkent Summit was held due to the efforts and initiative took by the Soviet Prime Minister Alexi Kosygin. Soviet Prime Minister was personally present to render such assistance as the two heads might require. The Tashkent Declaration was ultimately signed on January 1966.[25]

Thus, the Soviet Union took a lead in arranging a meeting between Prime Minister Lal Bahadur Shastri and President Ayub Khan of Pakistan. Under the Tashkent Declaration the two countries agreed to settle their disputes through peaceful methods. Within a few hours after Tashkent Declaration, Shashtri died of a massive heart attack. In fact, the whole world, except China, desired success at the Tashkent Summit. In the meeting both countries stood by their rigid positions. There was no progress for 6 days. The Under the Tashkent Declaration both the countres agreed to withdraw their forces to the position of 5 August 1965. The Tashkent Declaration, though did not lead to the settlement of the Kashmir problem, paved the way for settlement of disputes between India and Pakistan in a peaceful manner.

The Kashmir problem continued to strain the relations between the two countries even in the subsequent years. Despite serious efforts made by the United Nations and other powers, no mutually agreed solution of the problem has been found as yet. Prof. Michael Brecher has rightly said "Kashmir symbolises the root of the conflict between India and Pakistan. Here lies the last field of battle over the ideological cleavage which rent the subcontinent as under in 1947.[26]

2. The Canal Water Dispute : The question of sharing river waters has been another important factor in Indo-Pak relations. As a result of the partition of Punjab the problem of division of water of rivers cropped up. Under the 'standstill Agreement', India agreed to supply water to the canals in Pakistan. However, the 'Standstill Agreement' lapsed in April 1948, because Pakistan failed to renew the same. On May 4, 1948, India and Pakistan concluded another agreement which provided for progressive diminution of supplies to Pakistan by India. This treaty or agreement worked for about 2 years. During the next decade heated debates and negotiations continued regarding the distribution of river waters. Ultimately, through the good offices of the World Bank a treaty was signed in September 1960 by India and Pakistan which is popularly known as the 'Indus Waters Treaty'. In terms of this treaty India as not only agreed to allot the water of three western rivers—Indus, Jhelum and Chenab to Pakistan, but also agreed to supply water from the rivers–Ravi Beas and Sutlej on the Indian side. Pakistan was to be assisted by India and other countries in the construction of canals for link purposes. Thus, the dispute over canal waters was amicably settled.[27]

3. Pakistan and Military Alliances : As noted earlier, from the very beginning India had been opposed to the formation of military pacts and preferred to follow a policy of keeping aloof from the power bLoCs. It was therefore, natural that India reacted very sharply when Pakistan became member of the western military alliances and received military assistance from United States of America. It may be noted the US took initiative in the matter and offered military assistance to Pakistan with a view of strengthen the defence capabilities in the Middle East and South East Asia against communist threat. Pakistan became a member of the CENTO and SEATO in 1954.[28] India strongly reacted to these moves because India would have to compensatory measures at the expense of her economic development on which the future happiness of the country depended. The Indian objection was based on three grounds :

1. It would bring the cold war to the borders of India and disturb peace of the region for which India had been working so hard;
2. It would upset the balance existing between India and Pakistan which was dangerous for India;
3. It would introduce western and foreign domination into Asia in a new guise.

It may be noted that though the military alliances which Pakistan joined were primarily mean to meet the communist danger and were not directed against India, yet the arms made available to Pakistan a member of these alliances were bound to be used against India in case of a war. This was fully confirmed by the two wars of 1965 and 1971 when Pakistan openly used the arms supplied to her against India and United States could not keep any effective check on her inspite of the clear understanding given to India in this regard.[29]

4. Sino-Pak Agreement : The growing intimacy between Pakistan and China was another factor which strained the Indo-Pak relations. Pakistan could not develop good relations with China till 1962 partly because Pakistan was a member of the military alliances sponsored by the Western countries and partly because China maintained very friendly relations with India. However, after the China-Indian conflict of 1962 the two countries came closer to each other. China made available to Pakistan large amounts as interest free loans and also assisted her in the establishment of a number of industries. On her part, Pakistan agreed to surrender a large slice of Indian territory under her occupation to China. The intimate relations between Pakistan and China, two countries with different ideologies were made possibly by their common enemity towards India. This growing intimacy of Pakistan with China greatly strained her relations with India.

5. Revolt of Bangladesh : The revolt by the Bengalis of East Pakistan also contributed towards the straining of relations between India and Pakistan. In December 1970 elections were held in Pakistan which resulted in absolute majority for Sheikh Mujibs Awami League in provincial Assembly of East Pakistan. At the national level also his party secured a majority. However, under pressure from Bhutto, President Yahya Khan refused to Summon of the National Assembly. Consequently in March 1971, Sheikh Mujibur Rehman started a civil disobedience movement. A people's army known as 'Mukti Bahini' was also formed with a view to achieve freedom. The Pakistani military leaders resorted to suppression of people in East Bengal which resulted in large influx of Bengali refugees to India. These refuees crossed over to India in large number to escape persecution.[30] This not only caused seriouos strain of the economy of India but also strained her relations with Pakistan.

Further, the Government of Pakistan has not only refused to transfer power legally elected representatives, but has arbitrarily prevented the National Assembly from assuming its rightful and sovereign role. The people of East Bengal are being sought to be suppressed by the naked use of force, bayonets, machine guns, tanks, artillery and air craft. The Government and the people of India have always desired and worked for peaceful, normal and fraternal relations with Pakistan. The Indian Government ledged to develop friendly relations with the neighbouring countries and tried to give it concrete shape by encouraging closer relations with Pakistan.

The net result to the war was division of Pakistan and creation of sovereign state of Bangladesh which was recognised by India in December 1971. Sheikh Mujibur Rehman was released from Pakistani jail, but only after power was transferred in Pakistan from Yahya Khan to Z.A. Bhutto. The new President took credit for the release of Sheih though he himself was largely responsible for his arrest and detention. While going to Dhaka, Sheikh Mujibur Rehman stopped in Delhi and thanked India for its role in the independence of Bangladesh.[31]

The Shimla Accord

Zulfiqar Ali Bhutto assumed office of Chief Marshal Law Administrator and President on December 20, 1971. He was a leader of Pakistan people's party which had won 80 seats in the National Assembly elections held a year earlier. He inherited a mutilated Pakistan. As President, Bhutto made numerous promises including his 'determination' to reunite Bangladesh with Pakistan.[32] Several army commanders held responsible for Pakistan's defeat were removed from services and passports of many industrialists were seized.

After diplomatic level negotiations for several months, India-Pakistan Summit was held at Shimla in the end of June 1972. Mrs. Indira Gandhi and Mr. Z.A. Bhutto, assisted by their high level delegations, held complex and extensive discussions on various issues arising out of the war, as well as on general bilateral relations. After prolonged negotiations, Bhutto agreed on essentially a bilateral approach to Indo-Pak relations. The accord signed at the end of Shimla conference provided both the countries would work to end the conflicts and disputes between them and pledged to work for lasting friendship in the sub-continent. With these objectives in view, Indira Gandhi and Bhutto agreed to seek peaceful solutions to disputes and problems through bilateral negotiations and neither India nor Pakistan would unilaterally change the existing situation, and not to use force against each other, nor violate the territorial integrity, nor interfere in political freedom of each other.

The value of Shimla Agreement lies in the commitment of two countries to resolve all their disputes only through bilateral negotiations. Thus, Kashmir dispute would not be internationalised just as other disputes would also be resolved through direct negotiation.[33]

Indo-Pak Relations after Shimla Accord

The philosophy underlying Shimla Accord is bilateral approach to all the disputes between India and Pakistan. This point has been repeated innumerable times during 25 years since the Agreement was signed. Nevertheless, Pakistan did gain some ground after Shimla Accord. For example, Bhutto recovered the west Pakistan territory lost in the war. He got prisoners of war back without making much concession.

But Pakistan did get a set back in May 1974. India conducted its first and only, nuclear test in the Rajasthan desert in May 1974. India did not detonate a nuclear bomb. It was explosion of a device for peaceful use of nuclear energy, but it established India's capability to acquire a nuclear bomb. Z.A. Bhutto was shocked at India's nuclear test and said that Pakistan would never succumb to India's 'nuclear blackmail.'[34] He said that this test had put an end to the possibility of a no-war pact between India and

Pakistan. But India has been trying to convince the world that its nuclear programme is only for peaceful purposes. India has been asking the nuclear powers to destroy all their nuclear weapons also.

Zulfiqar Ali Bhutto was thrown out of power in 1977 in a military coup led by General Zia-Ul-Haq. He became President of Pakistan and held the office for over a decade. He was killed in an air crash in 1988. Zia had promised to hold elections for a new parliament within 90 days, but the elections were repeatedly put off Zia regime had put Bhutto under detention. He was tried for conspiracy and hanged to death. It was only after Zia's death that democracy was restored in Pakistan. Morarji Desai Government which came to power in 1977 tried hard to improve India's relations with all neighbours, particularly Pakistan. Several welcome gestures were made by both sides. Foreign Minister Atal Behari Vajpayee's visit to Pakistan in 1978 was highly successful and ice was broken. Pakistan later admitted that its relations with India were never better than those during 1977-79.

During Mrs. Gandhi's second tenure as Prime Minister (1980-84) and Rajiv Gandhi period (1984-89) several initiatives were taken but the Zia regime cleverly avoided to build confidence. On the contrary, it was widely believed that Zia regime took up itself the task of destabilising India by encouraging and assisting terrorism in Punjab for several years. Insurgency cost thousands of innocent lives in India. Mrs. Gandhi was assassinated in 1984, and this was also related to insurgency in Punjab. Rajiv Gandhi and Zia-Ul-Haq and later Rajiv and Prime Minister Benazir Bhutto initiated direct negotiations. Both sides referred to Shimla Accord and its commitment to bilateral approach. Nothing concrete resulted.[35]

The students took a very serious turn when Pakistan sponsored insurgency disturbed peace in the state of Jammu and Kashmir. The kidnapping of Rubaina Sayeed, daughter of the then Home Minister in late 1989 was the beginning of prolonged militancy in Kashmir. Rubaina's father Mufti Mohammed Sayeed, who hails from Kashmir, could get his daughter released only after hard bargaining with the militants. For nearly 7 years there was no elected government in the state. Only gun ruled the state, whether it was the gun of the militant or the gun of security man. In 1996, Legislative Assembly elections were held and after several years people elected an Assembly in which National Conference led by Dr. Farooq Abdullah emerged victorious. Dr. Abdullah's Government installed in October 1996 vowed to end militancy. Further, several rounds of talks at Foreign Secretary level were held between India and Pakistan during the Prime Ministership of P.V. Nara Simha Rao (1991-96). But Pakistan continued to encourage the separatist elements in Kashmir.[36]

During the seven year period (1989-96) of militancy, the economy of the Kashmir has been badly ruined. Tourist industry has completely ceased to function. Some foreign tourists were kindapped even killed. LoCal commercial activity was at a standstill as every now and then militants gave call for strike. Pakistan has been interested only in chaos. Pakistan was not interested in the well being and prosperity of Kashmir people. It talks of protection of Muslims, but militancy resulted in killing of several prominent Muslims as also large number of non-Muslims.[37] Further, thousands of Pandits fled from Kashmir and stayed as refugees in their own country in places like Jammu, Delhi etc.

Further, Indian Prime Minister I.K. Gujral had with his Pakistan counterpart Nawaz Sharif in May 1997 met during ninth SAARC Summit. The two leaders appeared to be determind to work seriously to find a solution to all the outstanding disputes between India and Pakistan. The two Prime Minister carefully avoided mention of Kashmir in all public statements and comments. When Mr. Vajpayee decided to go to Lahore by inaugural bus on February 20,

1999 he expected that his counterpart (Pakistani) would come to India in a reciprocal gesture. However, that did not happen.[38]

The Lahore Declaration

The Lahore Declaration emphasised that the two Prime Ministers shared "a vision of peace and stability between their countries and of progress and prosperity of their peoples." The Lahore Declaration contained all noble ideals of friendship, co-operation, non-interference, curbing terrorism and of good neighbours. The Lahore process was generally welcomed in India by the international community. The President Mr. K.R. Narayanan expressed the hope, soon after Vajpayee's return, and this visit would "mark a new chapter in bilateral ties." International community was also appreciative of the Lahore process.

Prime Minister Vajpayee assured Pakistan, during his Lahore trip, he called for "enduring peace, stability, progress and prosperity." The Prime Minister said, "We can change history but not geography, we can change our friends but not neighbours." However, he cautioned that a little spark could result in disasterous consequences and stressed the need for creating an atmosphere of confidence and mutual trust. He proved to be so correct. The Kargil conflict begun by Pakistan, soon after the Lahore visit, proved disasterous to the Indo-Pak efforts for friendship.[39]

The War in Kargil

Shimla Agreement or conference held in June 1972 was attended by Mrs. Indira Gandhi and Mr. Z.A. Bhutto to restore normalcy in the relation of two countries. The cease fire line with certain modifications, would be known as Line of Control. The armies of two countries would respect the LoC. The provision in the agreement was that the LoC would be respected by both the countries and that it would not be violated, all disputes would be resolved by the two countries through bilateral negotiations.[40]

The LoC was identified by senior military officers of India and Pakistan in 1972. The maps of which LoC was marked were duly signed by the officers of the two countries. For almost 27 years, the LoC was never violated. Indian authorities could not anticipate that Pakistan had the game plan of sending militants as well as its army regulars, in civilian clothes, to occupy the heights on Indian side of LoC in the Kargil sector. The Kargil sector is about 100 km in length. The Pakistan intruders invaded the LoC. It was only an aggression against India, but was also treacherous. The Kargil area was invaded by Pakistan intruders, militants as well as army regulars. The international community gave full support to Indian position. The USA, China also favoured Pakistan's withdrawal from Kargil International Community wanted India to exercise restraint, which India did. But the Pakistani intruders crossed the LoC, that resulted in heavy casualties as more than 400 Indian troops were killed. Pakistan suffered much heavier loss of its soldiers.[41] As its troops were beaten back, they left behind several hundred dead bodies including those of their regular troops. These bodies were then buried by Indian troops with proper religious rites.

It is true that over intelligence agencies failed to expect Pakistani entry into Kargil. Critics even said that the government ignored the warning signals. In May 1999 when Indian army supported by the air force launched "Operation Vijay" and finally defeated the enemy decisively. It was realised by the International Community that Pakistan had violated the LoC in Jammu and Kashmir by sending the intruders in Kargil sector of the state. By the end of 1999, cross border terrorism assumed new dimensions. In December, an Indian Airlines flight from Kathmandu to Delhi was hijacked by five armed men. This plane was eventually taken to Kandhar in Afghanistan. The area is controlled by Pakistan supported Taliban.[42] For seven long days more than 150 passengers and members of the crew were kept hostage on gun point. The hostage were released only when India agreed to release three of the militants detained in Indian jails. The hijackers were Pakistani nationals and they managed to go back to their country. India had enough evidence to show Pakistan's involvement in this crime. This further spoilt India-Pakistan relations.

Indo-China Relations

India's relations with China have been another important factor in her foreign policy. Infact, these relations antidate Indian Independence. India expressd full sympathy for China when she was subjected to Japanese aggression. After independence, India got so much pre-occupied with her own problems and China was pre-occupied with a civil war, that no intimate relations between the two could be cultivated.

The Problem of Tibet

The relations between India and China suffered a set- back when the Chinese leaders publically declared their intention to liberate Tibet. This was quite preturbing to India which considered the existence of Tibet as a buffer state as vital to her security. In October 1950, China despatched an army to liberate Tibet contrary to an understanding given to India that the issue would be resolved peacefully. Therefore, India lodged a protest with China. Dalai Lama wanted to raise the question of Tibet at the United Nations, but was prevented from doing so by the major world powers. Even India did not support this move because she did not want to condemn China at the international forum and seal all prospects of better relations with her. Ultimately an agreement was reached between China and Tibetan leaders on 23rd May 1951 which recognised full Chinese sovereignty over Tibet with limited Tibetan autonomy in certain matters. India's desire of full Tibetan autonomy within Chinese Suzerainty was not fulfilled.[43] The agreement promised 'Tibetan Autonomy' but provided that China would regulate Tibet's external relations, Chinese army would be posted in Tibet for defence, full respect would be given to the Dalai Lama, full religious freedom in Tibet, China would co-operate in Tibet's development the administrative and military mission of China would be based in Tibet. Thus, Tibet became for all purposes, a Chinese territory.

The Panchsheel Agreement

India was disappointed at China's Tibet policy. But it did not allow its friendship with China to be adversely affected. India continued to support China's demand for representation in the United Nations, not only at this stage but even during and after China's aggression on India in 1962. During the latter part of Korean Crisis (1950-53) China appreciated India's principled stand. Negotiations started for a comprehensive trade agreement between India and China. These resulted in the signing of an agreement by India and China concerning trade and intercourse between the "Tibet Region of China" and India. The agreement was signed on 29 April 1954, for a period of 8 years. India surrendered its extra-territorial rights in Tibet, and accepted China's full sovereignty over Tibet. Thus, it was accepted that Tibet was a region of China. India also surrendered its control over post and telegraph administration in Tibet.[44] The five principles of Panchsheel (see below) were also incorporated in the agreement. The Trade Agreement was followed by visits of Chinese Prime Minister Chou-En-Lai to India in June 1954 and of Prime Minister Nehru to China in October. The two Prime Ministers were warmly received in the host countries.

At the end of premier Chou's visit to New Delhi (June 1954), the Prime Ministers of India and China issued a Joint statement emphasising the five principles to guide and regulate the bilateral relations between the two neighbours. It formalised the famous five principles popularly known as the Panchsheel. The five principles are :

1. Mutual respect for each other's territorial integrity and sovereignty,
2. Mutual non-aggression,

3. Mutual non-interference in each other's internal affairs,
4. Equality and mutual benefit, and
5. Peaceful co-existence.

Nehru and Chou, besides reaffirming their faith in the five principles of Panchsheel, agreed that Tibet was a part of people's Republic of China. The five principles of Panchsheel were adopted by the Bandung Conference (1955) with minor modifications. The principles were later adopted by many countries as the basis of their bilateral relations. The four year period after signing the Panchsheel has been described as the years of 'Sino-Indian honeymoon' and of "Hindi-Chini Bhai-Bhai."[45]

Indo-China War, 1962

China revolted India on October 20, 1962. After the unilateral announcement of cease fire on November 21, 1962. The border war left a trail of bitterness. Mutual hostility dominated the Sino-Indian relations for nearly two decades.

Although embassies were functioning there were no full ambassadorial-level relations between the two countries during 1962-74. It was after quick negotiations that in April 1975, the then Foreign Minister Y.B. Chavan announced in the Lok Sabha that in a bid to improve relations, India had decided to send an Ambassador to China. India designated Mr. K.R. Narayanan, the former senior diplomat (Ex. President of India) as its ambassador to China. With the arrival of Chinese Ambassador in New Delhi diplomatic relations were normalised in 1975. But, exchange of ambassadors by itself was not detente. India being aggrieved party, waited for an initiative from China.[46]

The relations between India and China remained strained even after the two ambassadors took charge. Border was the only one of the many problems. Even today the relations remained strained.

Vajpayee's China Visit

The Ex-prime Minister Vajpayee visited China when he was the External Affairs Minister in February 1979. Vajpayee's discussions in Peking, three years after normalisation of diplomatic relations, were generally fruitful, except on the border issue.[47] Further goodwill missions were exchanged during 1981-83. Earlier, in 1978, after a high level trade delegation visited India. Ex-vice-President, B.D. Jatti also visited China in 1978 on the occasion of Chinese National Day.

Post-1980 Scenario

The initiative taken by Desai's Janata Government was utilised by Mrs. Gandhi when she returned to power in 1980. Hua Chinese PM and Indira Gandhi agreed to pursue the goal of improving relations. The Chinese Premier Li Peng paid a visit to India in December 1991, when Rao and Li Peng agreed to increase mutual co-operation. The basic obstacle in the improvement of Sino-Indian relations remained the border dispute and the problem of Tibet. Several rounds of official level talks, Indian Foreign Ministers visit to China PM Rajiv Gandhis visit and meetings of various Indian and Chinese leaders in international fora like Indira-Zhao meeting at Cancun, Li Peng Narasimha Rao meeting at Security Council Summit (1992) have borne no fruit.[48]

Prime Minister Narasimha Rao paid a return visit to China in 1993. During this visit the two countries agreed to keep the border dispute apart but develop friendly relations in other fields. China is keen to develop friendly relations with India. This is reflected in highest level visit in

November 1996 of China's President Jiang Zemin. Despite the end of Cold War, China maintained close military and political relations with Pakistan. In early 1960s, the motive behind China continued to associate itself with Pakistan's nuclear programme. Thus, it was a disturbing trend in India's foreign policy towards China.[49]

Agreement for Confidence Building Measures, 1996: In 1996 Prime Minister H.D. Deve Gowda met Chinese PM in Rome in November 1996 and he said India wanted to develop co-operative friendship with China. Taking the next step, India and China signed an agreement for confidence building in 1996. In June 1999 Mr. Jaswant Singh visited China for bilateral talks. The tradition of friendly relations between the two countries and their joint role in outlining the five principles of peaceful co-existence, which had since become model of international dealings.[50]

REFERENCES

1. Mahendra Kumar, Theoretical Aspects of International Politics, Agra, p. 352.
2. M.S. Rajan, Studies in India's Foreign Policy, New Delhi, p. 286.
3. K.P. Misra, The Conceptual Profile of Non-Alignment in Misra and Narayanan (ed.) Non-Alignment in Contemporary International Relations, p. 197.
4. *Ibid.*, p. 198.
5. V.P. Dutt, India's Foreign Policy, Vikas, New Delhi, p. 4.
6. Rajan, *op. cit.*, p. 287.
7. *Ibid.*
8. See V.N. Khanna, International Relations, Vikas, New Delhi.
9. Satish Kumar, Towards a Stronger and Democratic United Nations: India's Rule, in International Studies, April-June 1993, p. 174.
10. Foreign Minister of India January 80–July 84 and 1988-89.
11. M.S. Rajan, *op. cit.*, p. 175.
12. Werner Levi, Free India in Asia, p. 67.

13. K. Raman Pillai, India's Foreign Policy, New Delhi, p. 70.
14. Arguments analysed by Shri Ram Sharma in India's Foreign Policy (Hindi) pp. 166-167.
15. Kuldip Nayar, Distant Neighbours, pp. 61-62.
16. Michael Brecher, Nehru: A Political Biography, 1959, p. 577.
17. M.S. Rajan, *op. cit.*, p. 82.
18. V.P. Dutt, *op. cit.*, p. 186.
19. Rajan, *op. cit.*, p. 87.
20. Dutt, *op. cit.*, pp. 186-187.
21. Rajan, *op. cit.*, p. 147.
22. Dutt, *op. cit.*, p. 193.
23. V.P. Dutt, India's Foreign Policy, Vikas, New Delhi, p. 252.
24. *Ibid.*, p. 256.
25. On the occasion of Prince Birendra's marriage reciption.
26. V.P. Dutt, *op. cit.*, p. 233.
27. Chandrika Gulati, Liberation to Fundamentalism, New Delhi, p. 102.
28. *Ibid.*, p. 174.
29. Ministry of External Affairs Report, 1995-96.
30. V.P. Dutt, *op. cit.*, p. 323.
31. S.D. Muni, India and its Neighbours, in International Studies, JNU, 1993, p. 199.
32. *Ibid.*, p. 189.
33. Ministry of External Affairs Report, *op. cit.*, 1995-96.
34. Mahendra Kumar, *op. cit.*, p. 432.
35. M. Zuberi, Co-operative Denuclearisation, NPT Safeguards and India's Strategy, in International Studies, JNU, April-June, 1993.
36. *Ibid.*
37. Jasjit Singh, A Flawed Treaty in Savita Pande (ed.) India and the Nuclear Test Ban IDSA, p. 17.
38. V.P. Dutt, India's Foreign Policy, Vikas, New Delhi, p. 501.
39. *Ibid.*, p. 502.
40. *Ibid.*
41. Jasjit Singh, Extinguishing the Agni, Indian Express, 12, December, 1996.

42. *Ibid.*
43. *Ibid.*
44. The Times of India 14 December, 1996.
45. Jasjit Singh, A Flawed Treaty, *op. cit.,* p. 5.
46. Werner Levi, Free India in Asia, Mimeapolis, 1952, p. 85.
47. Jagat S. Mehta, India-China Relations, in V.A. Pai Pannandikar (ed.) India's Foreign Policy Problem, Vol. I p. 221.
48. B.M. Kaul, The Untold Story, New Delhi, p. 387.
49. People's Republic of China was given representation in the United Nations in 1971 itself.
50. J.N. Dixit, No Place for Emotionalism, Indian Express, 12 November 1996.
51. G.P. Deshpande, Looking into Next Millennium: India and China in International Studies, New Delhi, 1993.

6

India and the United Nations

Introduction

India's foreign policy recognises the United Nations as the humanity's hope for a peaceful and secure world order. The Constitution of India in Article 51, gives directive to the Government to promote international peace and seek peaceful settlement of international disputes. India endeavours to act on this principle. The United Nations is an organisation of sovereign nations dedicated to the cause of world peace and working for peaceful settlement of disputes and avoidance of war.[1] Faith in the United Nations and co-operation with the world body is an important principle of India's foreign policy. When India became independent in August 1947, it voluntarily decided to continue as an active member of the United Nations. India's commitment to the ideals of the United Nations was expressed time and again, without any reservations. During first 50 years of the existence of the United Nations, India always fulfilled its obligations, co-operated with all organs of the UN and its specialised agencies, and faithfully discharged such responsibilities as were assigned to it from time to time. These included India's role in peace keeping in West Asia and the Congo. India has actively co-operated with the UN in all its efforts for disarmament and arms control. However, India refuses to compromise with its basic values, principles and national interest. Before we discuss India's contribution in various spheres, by way of co-operation with the United Nations, a brief explanation of the formation of the United Nations, its objectives and membership will not be out of place.[2] A very brief account of major organs of the UN is also given.

Origin of the United Nations

The United Nations is described as the symbol of hope of the mankind. It is through this hope, peace is possible. The United Nations is an organisation of 185 Sovereign States. It was set up in October, 24, 1945 to replace the ill-fated League of Nations.

Objectives of the United Nations

The United Nations is "sharing in the name of solidarity." The mankind's hope and involvement is reflected in the preamble itself. It says, "We the people of the United Nations determined to save succeeding generations from the scourage of war, which twice in our lifetime has brought untold sorrow to mankind do hereby establish an international organisation to be known as the United Nations." Thus unlike the League of Nations, peoples of the world are source of power of the United Nations. Purposes of the United Nations are stated in Article 1 of the Charter. Briefly these purposes are :

1. to maintain international peace and security, and with that aim in view to take effective collective security measures for the prevention and removal of threats to peace,
2. to develop a friendly relations among nations,
3. to achieve international co-operation in solving economic, social, cultural and humanitarian problems, and
4. to be a centre for harmonising the actions of nations in the attainment of these common ends.

Thus, the United Nations is a necessity for maintenance of international peace, for protection of human rights, and for socio-economic development of the member-states.

Article 2 of the Charter lays down seven principles for the guidance of the UN and its members in pursuit of the above mentioned purposes. These are :

1. Sovereign equality of all the members of the UN,
2. all members shall fulfil in good faith the obligations assumed by them in accordance with the Charter,
3. peaceful settlement of international disputes so that international peace and security, and justice, are not threatened,
4. all members will refrain from threat or use of force against the territorial integrity of other states,
5. all members will give all possible assistance to the United Nations, and will not give any help to a country against whom the UN is taking action,
6. The UN will try to ensure that even non-members act in accordance with the principles of the Charter.
7. the United Nations shall not intervene in matters which are essentially within domestic jurisdiction of the states.

These principles sum up the objectives for which the UN was established. Thus, the sovereignty of nations is to be honoured, their integrity protected, disputed are to be peacefully resolved, use of force is to be avoided, and no action is to be taken by the UN in matters falling within the domestic jurisdiction of the states. All the provisions of the Charter revolve around the above mentioned purposes and principles.

Membership of the United Nations

Membership of the United Nations is open to all sovereign, peace-loving states of the world. According to Article 3 of the Charter, the countries who attended the San Francisco Conference, and those who had signed the United Nations Declaration on January 1, 1942 became original members of the United Nations. The number of such original members was 51. Later, according to Article 4, "all peace-loving states which accept the obligations contained in the present Charter," could be admitted as members of the UN. Admission of new members is effected by a decision of the General Assembly upon the recommendation of the Security Council. Accordingly, many countries who could not become members in 1945 were later admitted to the membership of the UN. Besides, a large number of countries who were colonies were admitted from time to time as they attained independence.[3] When Soviet Union disintegrated, all its Union Republics, who became sovereign states, were admitted. Now, the total number of members went up to 185.

Principal Organs and Specialised Agencies

A brief mention of principal organs of the UN and its specialised agencies will not be out of place. Six principal organs created by the UN Charter are :

1. The General Assembly,
2. Security Council,
3. Economic and Social Council,
4. Trusteeship Council,
5. International Court of Justice, and
6. The Secretariat.

The General Assembly being a plenary organ consists of all the (185) members of the United Nations. The General Assembly meets at least once a year, and can discuss any matter within the scope of UN Charter and may make recommendations to the members, or to the Security Council or direct to the Secretary General. It elects non-permanent members of the Security Council and has other electoral functions and functions related to international peace and co-operation.

The Security Council, consists of 5 permanent and 10 non-permanent members. The Security Council has the primary responsibility of maintenance of international peace and security. It performs important functions in the areas of pacific settlement of international disputes, initiates collective security measures and organised UN peace keeping activities.

The Economic and Social Council consists of 54 members elected by the General Assembly. It is responsible for socio-economic co-operation in the world. The ECOSOC cordinates the activities of several specialised agencies.

The Trusteeship Council was responsible for supervision of management of trust territories. These territories were either former mandates or new trust territories detached from Japan and Italy after their defeat in the Second World War. With the process of decolonisation having been completed the Trusteeship Council has ceased to be of much use.[4]

International Court of Justice is the Judicial organ of the UN. It has made up of 15 Judges elected from as many different countries. These eminent Jurists, as Judges of ICJ, seek to find just and fair solutions to legal disputes brought to the Court. It interprets international law. It also has advisory Jurisdiction and gives advice on matters of law to the UN General Assembly and the Security Council.

The Secretariat is the permanent office of the UN. It comprises a Secretary-General and such staff as the organisation may decide to have. The Secretary General is elected normally from a small power and is head of the international civil service. He acts as the Secretary General in General Assembly as well as the Security Council. He often brings disputes to the notice of the Security Council, and performs numerous political functions assigned to him by the two principal organs. Dr. Boutros-Ghali and Kofi Annan were elected as the Secretary General of the UNO for the period of 5 years.

The UN has several specialised agencies. These include—

1. Specialised Agencies concerned with technical matters, *viz.* International Civil Aviation

Organisation (ICAO), World Metrological Organisation (WMO), Universal Postal Union, and International Telecommunication Union.

2. Agencies engaged in social and humanitarian activities include International Labour Organisation (ILO), United Nations Educational, Scientific and Cultural Organisation (UNESCO), World Health Organisation (WHO), Food and Agriculture Organisations (FAO), and
3. Agencies that tackle international financial problems. These include—International Monetary Fund, International Bank of Reconstruction and Development (World Bank), and International Development Authority (IDA). India co-operates with most of these agencies and receives help and assistance from many of them. Two such prominent bodies are UNICEF (Children's Fund) and the United Nations Population Fund.

India's Role in the United Nations

India has actively co-operated with various principal organs and specialised agencies of the United Nations. India has served a member of 2-year terms as a non-permanent member of the Security Council. India's Mrs. Vijay Lakshmi Pandit was elected as President of the eighth session of the UN General Assembly. The grace and dignity with which she conducted the proceedings of the General Assembly received all-round acclaim.[5] India's association with the Economic and Social Council is almost permanent and it has offered such assistance in numerous socio-economic activities as it is capable of Eminent Indian Jurists, such as B.N. Rau and Nagendra Singh, have served with distinction as Judges of the International Court of Justice. Dr. Nagendra Singh was also President of the Court. Various specialised agencies have helped India overcome shortages and solve problems such as of health, malnutrition, food, child care etc. Nehru's faith in the United Nations and its reconstructive efforts remained the underlying principle of India's policy towards the United Nations, and seeking solution to various international problems through this organisation.

A brief discussion on India's contribution to the UN efforts is given below.

The issue of membership of several newly independent countries was one of the earliest issues that attracted India's concern. India fully supported the cause of admission of those sovereign states which were being denied admission. Their membership was blocked, in the context of Cold War, by one superior power or the other. These included Japan and a number of socialist countries. India led a group of developing countries whose support proved valuable in getting 16 countries admitted in 1956. India forcefully pleaded for representation of Communist China in the United Nations. India supported Chinese admission even after India was attacked by China in 1962. India argued that China as a large sovereign country could not be logically kept out of the world body.[6]

India pleaded strongly for speeding up the process of decolonisation in Asia and Africa. In such cases, as Indonesia where imperial powers tried to block their independence. India helped to build public opinion in favour of independence and quick decolonisation of Afro-Asia.

India came out strongly against the maintenance of colonial system. Prime Minister Nehru had argued that colonialism had to disappear so that the world could achieve peace, and "a friendly relationship" could develop between Asia and Europe. He believed that colonialism was obsolete in the contemporary world. The first major campaign that India initiated in the United Nations was aimed at forcing the Government of the Netherlands to give up its control over Indonesia. The conference of Indonesia conveyed by Prime Minister Nehru in New Delhi in January 1949 made significant contribution to the cause of Indonesia's independence which became a reality by the end of 1949.

India along with other like minded countries, played a significant role in the release of French colonies of Tunisia, Algeria and Morocco. India supported the cause of freedom of Cyprus. By 1960s most of the colonies had achieved independence. The policy of non-alignment movement was initiated by Nehru along with Egyptian President Nasser and Yugoslavia's Tito.

India had cut off diplomatic relations with South Africa in 1949. India fully supported the cause of independence of Namibia and co-sponsored resolutions in the United Nations calling upon South Africa to grant independence to Namibia. The freedom fighters of Namibia recognised Indian's contribution in the cause of their struggle when they finally won their statehood in 1990.

India is a strong supporter of the UN efforts for protection of human rights. Even since the United Nations General Assembly adopted the Universal Declaration of Human Rights in December 1948, India has co-operated in implementation of human rights related decisions and resolutions. The two human rights covenants have received India's wholehearted support. The Constitution of India, enacted 1949, incorporated most of the human rights either as fundamental rights or as directive principles of state policy. Wherever there is violation of human rights, India has raised its voice against such violation.[7] The human rights violation in South Africa is one such case in which India played a leading role in demanding end of all such violations. India either sponsored or, at least, supported resolutions passed by the General Assembly condemning apartheid in South Africa. Apartheid was declared to be a crime against humanity. India's role was highly appreciated by Dr. Nelson Mandela who became the first non-white President of South Africa in May 1994, after an all-party election returned him to power. Thus, India led the movement against apartheid both in the United Nations and outside it. India has constituted its own National Human

Rights Commission, chaired by a former Cheif Justice of India. This Commission is expected to ensure that there are no human rights violations in India. It also suggests measures to check violations and protect human rights in India.

India has played a consistently positive and energetic role in UN efforts for disarmament and arms control. India stands committed to total nuclear disarmament. India pleaded the cause of disarmament and arms control in Eighteen Nations Disarmament Committee, special sessions of the UN General Assembly and finally in Conference on Disarmament (CD). India had signed the partial Test Ban Treaty, but firmly resisted all pressures to sign the Non-proliferation Treaty and blocked the Comprehensive Test Ban Treaty (CTBT) in 1996.

India has always actively supported peace keeping activities of the United Nations. Peace keeping as a concept, though not spelt out in the Charter, has evolved over the years as an internationally acceptable way of controlling conflicts. UN directed forces have not been used to wage wars, but to control and resolve conflicts between states or communities within states. During the first 50 years of UN existence about 35 peace-keeping operations were organised. These included, in some cases, peace keeping forces, and in others military observer missions. As Chairman of Neutral Nations Repatriation Commission (NNRC) India performed the difficult task of repatriation of the prisoners of Korean War.[8] India also acted as Chairman of the International Commission for Supervision and Control in Indo-China under the Geneva Agreement of July 1954.

Another important assignment was peace-keeping operations in the Congo by the Indian Independent Brigade during 1960-63. As in case of Korea the Congolese assignment involved the use of Indian troops. The Republic of Congo (later the Republic of Zaire) became independent from Belgian rule in June 30, 1960. After Katanga was reintegrated in February 1963, phased withdrawal of UN troops began. The role of Indian peace-keepers was greatly appreciated.[9]

Peace-keeping in West Asia after Anglo-French-Israeli aggression on Egypt, over the Suez Canal nationalisation issue, was another case of India's contribution to the UN. Immediately after the cease fire on US Soviet initiative a United Nations Emergency Force (UNEF) was raised to supervise the observance of cease fire. The UNEF was constituted by a resolution of the General Assembly. Soviet Union, Israel as well as Egypt abstained, as the USSR argued that only the Security Council could set up such a force. The UNEF included contingents from Canada Denmark, Finland, Norway, Sweden, Brazil, Cambodia, India, Indonesia and Yugoslavia. All of them like India were considered neutral in the Suez-related crisis. The UNEF ensured observance of cease fire, evacuation of Sinai area and Gaza strip from the Israel and patrolled the 273 km long Egypt-Israel border.[10]

Fifty Years of the United Nations in India

India, as mentioned earlier, was one of the founder-member of the United Nations. During the 50 year period, since its independence, India has maintained close links with the world body. India has contributed to UN. Peace-keeping efforts and has also been a host of several UN agencies. There are country offices of as many as 18 agencies in New Delhi, and they have been working in close co-operation with Government of India as well as some of the non-governmental organisations (NGOs). India's concern for peace has been reflected in her repeated calls for disarmament and complete and comprehensive ban on nuclear and thermo-nuclear tests, though ironically she has not signed the nuclear Non-proliferation Treaty (NPT) of 1985, on the ground of the treaty being discriminatory in nature. On the same ground, India refused to endorse the

Comprehensive Test Ban Treaty (CTBT) as adopted by the UN General Assembly in 1996."

India herself is a developing country, and she has consistenty been a strong supporter of the UN activities of development in other developing countries. India is now the second largest donor to the United Nations Development Programme (UNDP), which is the central development funding agency of the UN system. The maximum funds are donated to UNDP by the Organisation for Economic Co-operation and Development (OECD).

We will briefly deal with some of the major areas of co-operation between India and the UN system. Gender inequality has been, and still is, a major global problem. As the Beijing Declaration of the Fourth World Conference on Women, 1995 noted, "Women comprise about half the world's population, perform about 2/3rds of its work, receive only 1/10th of its income and own less than one hundredth of world assets." This is pathetic. The conference declared, "We reaffirm our commitment to ensure full implementation of the human rights of women and of the girl child as inalienabale, integral and indivisible part of all human rights and fundamental freedoms." Over the years, several UN agencies have been supporting programmes to improve the quality of life for women in India, and more than 100 other countries. The most significant contributions for gender equality and main streaming women into development has been made by the UN agency UNIFEM (United Nations Development Fund for Women). It has been working in association in the UNDP and several non-governmental organisations in India.[12] For example, SEWA (Self-Employed Women's Association) in India has been dealing with the problem of home workers (domestic help). It has also set up social security schemes for the un-organised women workers. ILO has been supporting both these activities.

An important issue being addressed to in India is to empower women by the Panchayati Raj System. The

Government of India, assisted by UNDP and UNICEF (United Nations Children's Fund) has initiated massive country-wide training programme to equip about 8,00,000 women members of the Panchayats to manage local government effectively and transform them into effective agents of social change. Once considered "invisible" in the economy, women today are an important percentage of the country's workforce. Women's economic contribution was more accurately reflected in the 1991 census. The agencies such as UNFPA, WHO and UNICEF are working in India in the fields of maternal health, female contraception and populations initiatives.

In India UNDP implements its largest country programme spending about 40 million US dollars per year in assistance. Its assistance supports activities related to areas such as technology transfer for increased industrial productivity, agricultural development, energy and environment, transport, communication and social infrastructure.

Food and Agriculture Organisation (FAO) has been supporting projects in agricultural sector including support of agricultural education, advance research including modern technologies, hybrid ride production, integrated pest management, cong-term support in desert locust control and technical assistance to National Dairy Development and for increasing milk production. In the forestry sector, FAO supports of forestry research and education. It also assists State Forest Departments on human resource development, and to meet the objectives of forest conservation and management. FAO was supporting in 1995 the implementation of 48 projects, including 27 UNDP funded projects. It organised recruitment of Indian Specialists for FAO assignments in other countries, and placement of fellows from other, countries for training in Indian institutions. FAO has made very valuable contribution in helping India in boosting of agricultural production in the country. As against production of only 50 million tonnes of food grained in 1950, the country had achieved a record production of 189 million tonnes by 1994-95. India now ranks second in the world in wheat and rice production and first in the production of ground nuts.[13]. There has also been remarkable progress, thanks to FAO, in the production of sugar cane, cotton, poultry, milk, fish, vegetables and fruits. This has been made possible through in production of new technologies in the field of agriculture.

But, inspite of impressive growth, India's food grains output cannot feed its population reaching nearly 1 billion people. According to an estimate nearly 300 million people in India are unable to buy sufficient food to satisfy minimum calorie requirements. Therefore, agriculture development in India has to deal with three basic issues namely, meeting national food requirements, reversing resource degradation and poverty alleviation of its rural population. The World Food Programme of the UN has given assistance for "food for work" programme which helps the lowest paid workers on large intensive government projects. The World Food Programme (WFP) has enabled economically poor people in rural India to improve their own living conditions while participating in the overall development of the country.

Another agency that has an important mandate is the World Health Organisation (WHO). It directs and co-ordinates international health work within the family of th
United Nations. The WHO has been divided itself into
regional offices. Its South-East Asia Regional Office situ
in New Delhi promotes healthcare in co countries incl
India, Myanmar, Indonesia, Thailand, Nepal, Bhutan
Lanka. In this region small pox has been eradicate
of global programme. There are no longer
epidemics line cholera plague and maleria. With
support of WHO, India has aimed at health for
A.D. It has taken up massive programme to cor
HIV/AIDS problems. India remains a very ac
special partner of WHO.[14] A number of Ind

serving as member of WHO Advisory panels, Boards and Global Committees. A large number of foreign fellows continue to receive training in Indian medical institutes.

The World Food Programme (WFP) has been described as the food aid arm of the United Nations. In India, WFP has been supporting the government in handling the problems of poverty, hunger, malnutrition and illiteracy by directly helping the poor, the tribals, women and children. Almost all the beneficiaries of WFP projects live in remote rural areas. India had received by 1995 the commitment for assistance worth about one billion US dollars. WFP assistance to India concentrates on three major sectors. They are 1. tribal development through foresty, 2. integrated child development, and 3. rural development through irrigation, settlement and inland fisheries.[15] The WFP had begun its mission to eradicate hunger in 1963. Food aid is of particular significance to women who are mainly concerned with bringing up the children.

The United Nations Fund for Population Activities (UNFPA) established in 1969 works under the guidance of the ECOSOC. It is the largest international funded source of populations assistance world wide. It helps various governments in designing and implementation of their population programme.[16] UNFPA has supported India in population activities since 1974. During the 1991-95 period its programme in India, providing assistance of nearly 90 million US dollars was 1. upgrading the capacity as well as the quality of health and family welfare services in states with high birth, death and infant mortality rate, 2. increasing self-reliance in production of contraceptives, 3. to help strengthen and intensity information and awareness in support of population education, and 5. enhancing women's status by improving their literacy, promoting employment and income generating opportunities in selected areas. The major thrust of UNFPA in India is reproductive health including family planning and sexual health. It's programme includes emphasis on gender equality and empowerment of women.

An area directly related with population activities is the child care. The United Nations Children Fund (UNICEF—originally called UN International Children's Emergency Fund) has a unique mandate to work on behalf of children on the basis of need and without discrimination. It was awarded Nobel peace prize in 1965. The work of UNICEF is based on the premise that all children have rights, and that it is the legal obligation of state and society to ensure that these rights are actually enjoyed.[17] The convention on the Right of the child adopted by the UN General Assembly in 1989 provides for legal and moral framework for UNICEF's work for children. The Articles of the convention on the Rights of the child have now become basis of UNICEF's work in India. The United Nations Children's Fund (UNICEF) now supports and funds in India programmes for children in primary health care, water supply and sanitation, primary education, nutrition and child development.[18] UNICEF is seeking ban on child labour, particularly in the case of carpet industry which is highly injurious to the health of child workers.

The United Educational, Scientific and Cultural Organisation (UNESCO) is an important specialised agency of the UN system. It is mainly concerned with education. In the field of science and technology, UNESCO seeks to respond to the needs expressed by Member States. It recognises importance of communication for development.[19] It also ensures translation of certain master pieces of world literature and recording of traditional music from all regions of the world. The New Delhi office of UNESCO covers 11 countries of South and Central Asia including Afghanistan, Pakistan, Maldives, Nepal and Myanmar.

In the field of education, learning without Barriers is a major step taken to help lower the barriers to education and to create an open flexible learning environment. UNESCO office in New Delhi has given special attention to education of girls and women, distance education and open schooling. It provides funds and assistance for the preservation of tangible and intangible heritage to protect the Indian culture.[20]

The Constitution of UNESCO declares that, "Since wars begin in the minds of men, it is in the minds of men that the defences of peace must be constructed." It is with this aim in view that the UNESCO concentrates on proper education for all round development of personality of the children as well as adults.[21] To achieve Education for All (EFA) in India more than 20 million children in 6-14 age group (of whom 60 per cent are girls) must be reached by the end of twentieth century. To achieve this aim, UN agencies including UNDP, UNFPA, UNESCO, UNICEF and the World Bank are assisting India in her efforts to reach her literacy and education targets.[22]

Humayun's Tomb and the Qutab Minar in Delhi are among the sites which have been included in the UNESCO's World Heritage List. Another unique project which addresses the interface between development and culture aims to assist the Indira Gandhi National Centre for the Arts in demonstrating "how fragments of the cultural past can be recreated", to promote inter-relationships between culture, environment and development.[23]

The UNESCO is committed to help India and other developing countries to ensure that education reaches all, and particularly the girl child. As an Algerian reformer A Ibn Badis had said, "Teach a boy and you will train one individual. Teach a girl and you will train the whole nation." It is with this ideals that the UN system in India has been working for education for all, and gender equality especially in the field of education employment.[24]

The International Monetary Fund (IMF) established in 1944 as part of Bretton Woods regime now has about 180 members. It seeks to ensure exchange of stability and orderly exchange arrangements among member countries. In addition, lately it has widened its scope and tries to establish a dynamic World economy.[25] The IMF provides financial assistance to countries experiencing balance of payment difficulties. India has been a member and beneficiary of IMF since 1945. IMF supported the stabilisation and structural reform programme that India embarked upon in 1991 with the aim of liberalisation of economy. India, thus, tried to become an active participant in World wide economic changes, openign up, accepting foreign investment and promoting market economic forces to operate freely.[26]

International Civil Aviation Organisation (ICAO) is another agency of the UN. It aims are to develop the principles and techniques of international air navigation and to foster the planning and development of international air transport. India is a member of ICAO, which establish regional air-navigation plans, creates standards and helps with aviation security, streamlines customs, immigration and public health formalities, and drafts air-law convention.[27]

Thus, these and other agencies of the United Nations are working in co-operation with the Government of India. It is a two-way co-operation. India has full faith, as a matter of policy, in the United Nations and its objectives, aims and goals of international peace and security, peaceful settlement of disputes, all round social and economic development, education and health for all. India has always co-operated with numerous activities of the UN and its agencies. In return, India has greatlely benefited from numerous agencies and funds provided by such bodies as UNDP, UNFPA, UNICEF, FAO, WHO, IMF and the World Bank.[28]

INDIA AND THE SAARC

Introduction

The setting up of the South Asian Association of Regional Co-operation (SAARC) marked the beginning of regional co-operation in South Asia. It has been described as one of the most important developments of 1980s in this region. This is a process that links several nations of the region in collective decision-making system. Joseph Nye has said that the process of integration implies recognition of mutual obligations and common interests. Both at the social and political levels human relationships have generally been in conflict.[29]

International relations are dominated by conflict and war which is a regular phenomenon. Conflicts tend to perpetuate. Even co-operation, the opposite of conflict, is often aimed of securing advantage in a situation of conflict. The conflicts are largely responsible for halting the developmental processes, which in turn leads to improverishment of the people. Therefore, the remedy for conflict lies in substituting it with Co-operation. Regional Organisations enable nation-states in a particular region to minimise their conflict and promote co-operation. The process of regional integration is translated into institutional framework through the regional organisations.[30]

Co-operation among states is promoted by common factors which may be geographic, ethnic, linguistic, religious, civilisational, politico-historical or socio-economic. The greater the interaction, the better are the chances of success of co-operative endeavours. The South-Asian region certainly has commonality of above mentioned factors, with minor variations.[31]

These factors have existed for a long time, but the concept of regional socio-economic and political co-operation is of recent origin. In South Asia it was only in 1977 that the idea of a regional organisation was first floated by the then Bangladesh President Zia-Ur Rehman. Several regional organisations in different parts of the world had already come into existence and were working fairly satisfactorily. These included the organisation of American States (OAS) Setup in 1948, the Arab League established in 1945, the

Association of South-East Asian Nations (ASEAN) setup in 1967, and the European Union (EU). The European Union in its present form was established in 1993. It evolved from the six-nation European Coal and Steel Community Created in 1952. This 15-member union is the most perfect and effective of all regional organisations.[32]

Article 52 of the Charter of United Nations provides for regional organisations. Some of the regional organisations established after IInd World War were of the nature of military alliance. These included North Atlantic Treaty Organisation (NATO) 1949, South East Asia Treaty Organisation (SEATO) (1954), the inter-American Defence System (1948), the Australia New Zealand. United States Pact (1952), CENTO (1959) and Worsaw Pact. In addition to defensive organisations, a number of functional organisations are also now is existence. These include European Union, ASEAN, APEC and SAARC.[33]

Origin of the SAARC

The South Asian Association of Regional Co-operation (SAARC) was established in December 1985 at a Summit of seven heads of states or governments, of South Asian countries, held at Dhaka. Initiative for SAARC was taken in 1977 by the then President of Bangaldesh Zia-Ur-Rehman. It was with the yearning to bring some measure of stability and peace, and to improve the sub-human conditions of eternal poverty and misery of new born Bangladesh that President Zia-Ur Rehman mooted the idea of regional co-operation in the immediate surroundings. It has been argued that compulsions of domestic conditions of economic chaos made Zia-Ur-Rehman suggest a regional organisation for economic co-operation.[34]

India and Pakistan, the two major actors of the region, were initially reluctant to join. Zia's proposal found ready acceptance by Sri Lanka, Nepal, Bhutan and Maldives. But Pakistan felt that an association where India would play or major role was not in its interest. The feeling in Pakistani circles was that India would dominate by sheer weight and size of everything—land, economy, military, industry, power, infrastructure, science and technology. Pakistan's attitude has always been "Never say yes to India." India is a giant among Lilliputs. However, India wanted to avoid playing a 'local big brother.' However, reluctance of both India and Pakistan was soon overcome by the desire for social, economic and cultural co-operation within the region.[35]

India, Pakistan, Bangladesh, Nepal, Bhutan, Sri Lanka and Maldives are the seven original members of the SAARC. Gunnar Myrdal had said about South Asia in 1968," there is a similarity in the basic economic conditions of the South Asian countries. All are very poor in general the largest are the poorest. This unfortunate situation has largely remained unchanged, though with economic liberalisation since 1991 future appears to be brighter. In 1994, according to the Human, Development Index, covering 173 countries, India ranked 135 and Pakistan 132 in terms of human development. This is pathetic. There has been growing redisation that co-operation at regional level can go a long way in areas such as poverty alleviation. Lack of co-operation can perpetuate economic misery inspite of liberalisation.[36]

Inspired by the then president Zia-Ur-Rehman, who had mooted the idea of SAARC, while touring India, Pakistan, Nepal and Sri Lanka in 1977, the Government of Bangladesh circulated a working paper, titled "Regional Co-operation in South Asia", advocating regional co-operation in economic, technical, scientific, social, cultural and educational fields. It was circulated in 1980 and it suggested that meetings at Foreign Secretary level should examine prospects of regional co-operation. From 1977 to 1981, consultative and preparatory work had been done.

The proposal was formally submitted to concerned governments in May 1980 by president Rehman. The first meeting of Foreign Secretaries was held at Colombo in April

1981. It was followed by six more such meetings in other capitals. Foreign ministers of 7 countries also held a number of meetings, before the Dhaka Summit.

An Integrated Programme of Action (IPA) was adopted in 1983 at Foreign Minister's meeting in New Delhi. The programme was announced through the New Delhi Declaration. During negotiations, leading to Dhaka Summit (1985), it was agreed tht SAARC would actively try for greater regional co-operation on the basis of sovereign equality of states, protection on the basis of territorial integrity, and non-interference in the internal affairs of each other. The co-operation was likely to grow in the economic, social and cultural spheres. Initially 11 areas of regional co-operation were identified. They were telecommunication, meteorology, transport, shipping, tourism, agricultural research, Joint ventures, market, promotion, scientific and technological co-operation, educational and cultural co-operation. These areas were quite vast to promote co-operation and seek regional unity.[37]

The spade work for launching the SAARC was completed in the Foreign Ministers meetings held at Male in July 1984, and Thimpu in May 1985. It was decided to hold a Summit of Seven South Asian Countries at Dhaka on December 7-8, 1985. The Summit was presided over by Bangladesh President General H.M. Ershad. India was represented by Prime Minister Rajiv Gandhi. The other heads of State who attended Dhaka Summit included president (Gen.) Zia-Ul-Haqob Pakistan, President Jayawardene of Sri Lanka, Kings of Nepal and Bhutan and President Mr. Abdul Gayoom of Maldives. The Dhaka Summit was held in a very cordial atmosphere. Sri Lanka's President Jayawardene praised the role of Late Mrs. Indira Gandhi and Prime Minister Rajiv Gandhi in the establishment of SAARC and promotion of regional co-operation, despite tensions and literal disputes. Jayawardene went to the extent of suggesting that Rajiv Gandhi should be requested to lead the Association. A ten point Charter of SAARC was adopted, and SAARC was formally launched.

It was decided and incorporated in the character that literal issues or disputes shall not be raised or discussed in the SAARC fora. Secondly, it was agreed to establish a permanent secretariat of the organisation. It details were to be worked out by the Foreign Ministers. The secretariat was temporarily located in Dhaka and Mr. Abdul Hasan was chosen as the SAARC Secretary-General. The Foreign Ministers later decided to establish the permanent Secretariat at Kathmandu (Nepal) where it now functions.

Objectives and Principles of SAARC

The Charter of the SAARC has spell out the following main objectives of the organisation :

1. To promote the welfare of peoples in South Asian Countries and to improve their quality of live;
2. To accelerate economic growth, social progress and cultural development,
3. To promote and strengthen collective self-reliance,
4. To contribute to mutual trust, understanding and appreciation of one another's problems,
5. To promote mutual assistance in the economic, social, cultural, technical and scientific fields,
6. To strengthen co-operation with other developing countires,
7. To strengthen co-operation among themselves in international fora, and
8. To co-operate with other regional and international organisations.

The principles of SAARC, as defined in its Charter are :

1. Regional co-operation through SAARC shall be based in mutual respect for the principles of sovereign

equality, territorial integrity, political independence, non-interference in internal affairs of other states and mutual benefit.

2. Such co-operation shall not be a substitute for bilateral and multi-lateral co-operation, but shall complement them, and
3. Such co-operation shall not be inconsistent with bilateral and multi-lateral obligations. Thus, the emphasis is or regional co-operation without interference either in bilateral or multi lateral obligations and without disregarding sovereign equality, or challenging territorial integrity and independence of all its members.[38]

Institutional Framework

The institutional framework of SAARC is based on direct involvement of heads of states or governments, foreign ministers and foreign secretaries of all the member-nations. At the lowest level there are a number of technical committees which are constituted for implementation of programmes and determining areas of co-operation along with all their financial and administrative implications. The technical committees are made up of officials and experts from various member-countries. They submit their reports to the Standing Committees. Next, there is a Standing Committee of Foreign Secretaries. It meets at least once a year, but may meet frequently. The Standing Committee monitors co-ordination, mobilised resources and identifies new areas of co-operation of the foreign ministers and the summit. It reviews the works of all the Technical Committees, receives their reports and considers them.[39] It issues guidelines for effective working of the technical committees. Next, the Foreign Ministers constitute a council of ministers, or Foreign Minister's Conference. It generally meets twice a year, though atleast one meeting a year is mandatory.

It reviews the progress of regional co-operation and grants political approval to the recommendations of the standing committee. The Foreign Ministers prepare agenda for the Summit and finalise measures to be discussed and declarations to be adopted by heads of states or governments in their annual Summit. Lastly, at the highest level are the annual Summits of heads of states or Governments. The summits are held in different countries and they consider reports of the Foreign Ministers. The Summits have political significance as they are the highest forum of South Asian Regional Co-operation. The financial resources are provided by member countries. Nine Summits were held during the first 12 years. Male Summit of 1997 was the last of these Summits.

After the end of Cold War, the single most critical problem faced by the world is that of development and under-development. Thus East-West divide has been replaced by the divide between rich and developed North and the poor and developing south. No other region in the world is more underdeveloped than South Asia, and none has more poverty and exploding population. At the same time no other region has comparable commonality in terms of geography, civilisation and ethno-linguistic affiliations. Yet, South Asia was the last of regional entities to have opted for regional economic co-operation.Yet, there are lots of expectations and there is a hope that South Asian countries will overcome their prejudices and work together for prosperity of the region.[40]

Expanding the SAARC

At the time of exploring the possibilities of a regional organisation for South Asia in 1977, a suggestion was made to include, besides the 7 who constitute SAARC, Iran, Afghanistan and Burma also. However, during the 8 years that were spent in planning and setting up the SAARC, the opinion centred around India, Pakistan, Nepal, Bhutan, Bangladesh, Sri Lanka and Maldives. After the formal establishment of SAARC in 1985, Afghanistan and Burma were sounded to join the Association. India was in favour of Afghanistan joining the SAARC, but Pakistan was obviously unhappy about Afghanistan joining the SAARC.[41]

In 1996, Mr. I.K. Gujral, Indias External Affairs Minister in Deve Gowda Government, called for the expansion of SAARC. Gujral himself became a Prime Minister in 1997. It was not easy to expand the organisation on such a large scale. Afghanistan in 1996 was too deeply involved in civil war, and to expect that country to respond to the call of SAARC would be unrealistic. As for Burma it was expecting an early membership of the Association of South-East Asian Nations (ASEAN). Therefore, late in 1996, it appeared that Burma may not be really interested in the membership of SAARC.

India, Pakistan and SAARC

Pakistan's policy of "hate India" is reflected in all its actions. Pakistan refuses to recognise India's secular character and cannot forget that Jinnah's two-nation theory was responsible for the creation of Pakistan. Communal divide is the basis of Pakistan's policy. It keeps its anti-India propaganda going, on the ground that Muslim-Kashmir must not remain a part of India. Pakistan has tried to raise the Kashmir issue at SAARC conferences. It even tried to have India censured in the 1996 conference on Human Rights at Vienna. The political problems between India and Pakistan are rooted in differing perception of common past of the sub-continent. This had been vitiating not only Indo-Pak bilateral relationship but also of SAARC framework.[42]

The most important problem between India and Pakistan are related to the sharing of Ganga waters. Yet, the two countries see the imperative of expanding trade relations between them. SAARC, whose foundation was laid by Bangladesh President, provides a forum to Bangladesh to project itself as a state determined to further the cause of regional co-operation in South Asia.

Nepal's system of government has changed (1990) from absolute monarchy to constitutional monarchy with a multiparty parliamentary democracy. Nepal's development depends upon how effectively it can profit from a preferential treatment it has received for 200 years from India.

Nepal's co-operative relations with India are a great help to the effectiveness of SAARC. While relations between India and Bhutan and India and Maldives have been very cardial, there has been the ethnic problem in Sri Lanka-India relations. India has played a leading role in the development of Bhutan and has received fullest co-operation from the country inhabited by 6 lakh people.

Prospects of SAARC

The utility of regional co-operation is now universally accepted. Such a co-operation in South Asia is also imperative, particularly because 50% of international trade is now being done at international level. Besides a wide commonality of factors also exists in South Asia. But, the attitude of Pakistan towards India and hostility in Indo-Pak relations is a major stumbling block. It is essential for any meaningful regional economic co-operation that it should be done both at inter governmental level as well as at people to people level.

There are a number of bilateral problems in South Asia. They must not be allowed to come in the way of regional co-operation. Development without detriment to their integrity and sovereignty is in the national interest of all the South Asian countries. It has been said that unlike the G-7 (Group of seven highly industrialised nations), we are P-7 (Group of poor seven of South Asia). We will have to remove the label of P-7. Though poverty is not a sin, yet to perpetuate it and accept it as a curse of destiny is harmful, and we must work for the change. This can be done through systematic develoment.[43]

The birth of SAARC was not related to bloc politics. It was considered a basic, inescapable, prerequisite for ensuring better living standards for millions of people. It was a bold political experiment involving seven nations with different political systems. It was an honest attempt at self improvement accepting the reality as start point.

Regional co-operation, which is being promoted everywhere, will be immensely useful in South Asia also. South Asian nations can enhance their bargaining power, through SAARC, with the developed North, and reduce their dependence on it. It will also create a new set of equitable relations within themselves in the region. "Being more inward looking, the South Asian nations can exploit the regional resources more effectively in an environment of mutual trust and co-operation." But, bilateral issues are largely responbile for slow progress in SAARC. Besides, there is some sort of hidden fear about India's position in the region. India alone has 72 per cent of South Asian territory and about 77 per cent of total population. This enables it to a position of hegemony, though India has no desire to impose its will on smaller neighbours.[44]

Among the conflicts that are creating difficulties in the region are ethnic tensions between Assamee and Bangladeshis, Tamils and Sinhalese, and Mohajirs and Sindhis in Pakistan.

Attempts will have to be made for ethnic and religious harmony. The issue of distribution of Ganga waters between India and Bangladesh has been amicably and permanently settled in order to accelerate Indo-Bangla co-operation. India-Pakistan conflct relating to Kashmir and occasional alleged encouragement of terrorism from across the border has been dominating politics in South-Asia. A report by the American Republic Party Task Force on Terrorism confirmed Pakistani efforts, with some Arab support, to destabilise India. Similar conclusion was reached in the American state Departments annual report for 1994 titled patterns of Global Terrorism.[45] The spirit of regional co-operation demands fruitful bilateral dialogues to resolve differences and promote development through co-operation. Distrust must be replaced by mutual understanding. There is ample scope of regional co-operation which can go a long way in promoting peace and progress in the entire world. In strengthening SAARC and making it more effective, the most important role has to be played by India. While all bilateral relationships are important, the most important and relevant in the future evolution and success of SAARC would be a rapproachement between India and Pakistan. Then alone SAPTA experiment will succeed and then alone path for SAFTA will be cleared.[46]

The Ninth Summit of SAARC held at Male, the capital of Maldives in May 1997 made a lofty declaration that poverty should be eradicated by the year 2000 A.D. in South Asia, which accounts for nearly one fifth of total population of the globe and has the largest number of poor in any region of the world. Nobody, however, explained how this gigantic task would be achieved in four years. The Declaration only said that "trade and tariff barriers militating against greater cross country flows" would be gradually reduced. The Summit declared the year 1997 as the "SAARC year of participatory Governance."[47] The seven heads of state or government at Male also emphasised the need for bringing women into the main stream of socio-economic development in the region. Besides, concerned about the promotion of child welfare in South Asia, it was decided to launch the SAARC decade of the rights of the child, from the year 2001 and 2010 A.D. The Summit also resolved to combat the nefarious activities such as terrorism and drug trafficking which posed serious threat to security and stability of member states.[48]

Regional co-operation in South Asia will eventually strengthen non-alignment. As major S.P. Yadav concludes, "It will provide an effective forum to deal with the rest of the world. It will consolidate the common desire to live and let live, strengthen the friendship, reconcile or minimise differences, and safeguard their independence and sovereignty. It will be the beginning of the new economic and political order in South Asia." There is no truth in the fear that India will dominate or establish its hegemonry.[49] In fact, regional co-operation is as much in India's national interest as in others. It will hasten development and promote political understanding.[50]

REFERENCES

1. N.D. Palmer and H.C. Perkins, International Relations. The World Community inTransition (Calcutta, 1970), Ist Indian reprint of the 3rd edn. 1970, p. 460.
2. Werner Levi, Foreign Policy, The Shastri Era, in K.P. Misra (ed.) Studies in Indian Foreign Policy (Delhi 1975), p. 158.
3. Quincy Wright (edited), The World Community (Chicago, University of Chicago Press, 1948).
4. N.D. Palmer, *op. cit.,* p. 472.
5. Werner Levi, *op. cit.,* p. 160.
6. K.P. Misra, *op. cit.,* p. 175.
7. H.J. Morgenthau, Politics Among Nations, p. 156.
8. See Henry Kissinger, Nuclear Weapons and Foreign Policy (New York, 1957), p. 142.
9. H.J. Morgenthau, *op. cit.,* p. 157.
10. H. Kissinger, *op. cit.,* p. 162.
11. See John H. Herz, International Politics in the Atomic Age, p. 67.
12. See E.H. Carr, The Twenty Year's Crisis 1919-39 (London, 1949), p. 232.
13. J.H. Herz, *op. cit.,* p. 69.
14. E.H. Carr, *op. cit.,* p. 75.
15. See Harold Nicolson, The Congress of Vienna (New York, 1946).
16. John W. Burton, International Relations (Cambridge, 1965), p. 58.
17. H. Nicolson, *op. cit.,* p. 130.
18. J.W. Burton, *op. cit.,* p. 138.
19. A.F.K. Organski, World Politics (New York, 1958), pp. 292, 297, 316-38.

20. J.H. Herz, International Politics in the Atomic Age, p. 154.
21. See Kenneth Waltz, International Structure, National Force and World Power, p. 130.
22. Kenneth Waltz, *op. cit.,* p. 135.
23. See Vernon Van Dyke, International Politics (New York, 1957).
24. Walter Lippmann, U.S. Foreign Policy : Shield the Republic (Boston, 1943).
25. See George F. Kennan, American Diplomacy 1900-1950 (Chicago, 1952), p. 100.
26. Raymond Aron, The Quest for a Philosophy of Foreign Affairs (Englewood Cliffs, 1960), p. 88.
27. Kenneth N. Waltz Man, the State and War (New York, 1959), p. 88.
28. See Karl Mannheim, Ideology and Utopia (New York 1936), p. 50.
29. See Karl Mannheim, *op. cit.,* p. 55.
30. John Stoessinger, The Might of Nations—World Politics in Out Time (New York, 1969), p. 24-25.
31. From the 1914 Conflict Study Seminar, Unpublished Reports.
32. Kenneth E. Boulding, Conflict and Defence (New York, 1962), p. 50.
33. See Kenneth E. Boulding, *op. cit.,* p. 60.
34. See Kenneth E. Boulding, Conflict and Defense, p. 55.
35. Thomas C. Schelling, The Strategy of Conflict (Cambridge Mass, 1960), p. 135.
36. Kessing's Contemporary Archives, 1951, p. 112.
37. See Balraj Puri, China and Indian Policy Easton World, 13 (September 1959), p. 30.
38. G. Barraclough, Survey of International Affairs, 1956-58, p. 335.
39. *Ibid.,* p. 340.
40. *Ibid.,* p. 345.
41. B.A. Prasad-India's Role in the Future of SAARC, in Strategic Analysis, Delhi, February 1995, p. 130.
42. Lt. Col. K.S. Ramanathan–India and the Future of SAARC, U.S.I. Journal, 1994.
43. Gunnar Myrdal Asian Drama, 1968, p. 46.

44. Nancy Jetley India and SAARC in World Focus, New Delhi, July 1996.
45. B.A. Prasad, *op. cit.,* p. 30.
46. Lt. Col. K.S. Ramanathan, *op. cit.,* p. 70.
47. Major S.P. Yadav : India's Role in the Future of SAARC, U.S.I. Journal, 1994.
48. Quoted in Prasad, *op. cit.,* p. 340.
49. S.D. Muni : Expanding SAARC in World Focus, New Delhi, July 1996.
50. B.A. Prasad, *op. cit.,* p. 38.

Selected Bibliography

BOOKS

APPADORAI, A. and ARORA, V.K., *India in World Affairs, 1957-58,* Sterling Publishers, New Delhi, 1975.

BAINS, J.S., *India's International Disputes : A Legal Study,* Asia Publishing House, Bombay, 1962.

BANDYOPADHYAYA, JAYANTANUJA, *Indian Nationalism versus International Communism : the Role of Ideology in International Politics,* Firma K.L. Mukhopadhyaa, Calcutta, 1966.

__________ *Social and Political Thought of Ganhi,* Allied Publishers, Bombay, 1969.

__________ *Mao Tse-tung and Gandhi : Perspectives on Social Transformation,* Allied Publishers, Bombay, 1973.

BARGHOORN, F.C., *Soviet Foreign Propaganda,* Princeton University Press, 1964.

BARKER, ERNEST, *National Character and the Factors in its Formation,* Methuen, London, 1948.

BARKES, R.N. and BEDI, M.S., *The Diplomacy of India,* Stanford University Press, 1958.

BELOFF, MAX, *Foreign Policy and the Democratic Processes,* Johns Hopkins Press, baitimore, 1963.

BERDING, A.H., *The Making of Foreign Policy,* Washington D.C., 1966.

BLACK, EUGENE, *The Diplomacy of Economic Development,* Harvard University Press, 1961.

BRECHER, MICHAEL, *India and World Politics : Krishna Menon's View of the World,* Oxford University Press, London, 1961.

__________ *Nehru : A Political Biography,* Oxford University Press, London, 1959.

CAMPBELL-JOHNSON, ALAN, *Mission with Mountbatten,* Robert Hale, London, 1951.

COLLINS, LARRY and LAPIERRE, DOMINIQUE, *Freedom at Midnight,* Vikas, New Delhi, 1979.

DALLIN, D.J., *Soviet Espionage,* Yale University Press, 1955.

DALVI, BRIG. J.P., *Himalayan Blunder,* Thacker & Co., Bombay, 1969.

DAS GUPTA, J.B., *Indo-Pakistann Relations,* Amsterdam, 1958.

DULLES, A.W., *The Craft of Intelligence,* Harper & Row, New York 1963.

DUTT, SUBIMAL, *With Nehru in the Foreign Office,* Minerva Associates, Calcutta, 1977.

EDRMAN, H.L., *The Swatantra Party and Indian Conservatism,* Cambridge University Press, 1967.

ERHMANN, H.W., *Interest Groups on Four Continents,* University of Pittsburg Press, 1958.

FAINSOD, M., *How Russia is Rules,* Harvard University Press, 1963.

FALK, R.A., and MENDLOVITZ, S.H. (eds.), *The Strategy of World Order,* World Law Fund, New York, 1966.

FRANKEL, J., *The Making of Foreign Policy : An Analysis of Decision-Making,* Oxford University Press, 1963.

GALBRAITH, J.K., *Ambassador's Journal : A Personal Account of the Kennedy Years,* Hamish Hamilton, London, 1969.

GUJRATI, B.S. (ed.), *A Study of Lal Bahadur Shastri,* Sterling Publishers, New Delhi, 1965.

GUPTA, SISIR, *India and Regional Integration in Asia,* Asia Publishing House, Bombay, 1964.

__________ *Kashmir : A Study in Indo-Pakistan Relations,* Asia Publishing House, Bombay, 1966.

HARRISON, SELIG S., *India : the Most Dangerous Decades,* Princeton University Press, 1960.

HEIMSATH, CHARLES H. and MANSINGH, SURJIT, *A Diplomatic History of Modern India,* Allied Publishers, Bombay, 1971.

HEVESY, PAUL DE, *The Unification of the World,* Pergamon Press, Oxford, 1966.

HERZ, JOHN, *Political Realism and Political Idealism,* University of Chicago Press, 1951.

INDIAN COUNCIL OF WORLD AFFAIRS, *India and the United Nations,* Manhattan Publishing Co., New York, 1957.

__________ *Defence and Security in the Indian Ocean Area,* Asia Publishing House, Bombay, 1958.

ISRAEL YAN, V., and others, *Soviet Foreign Policy : A Brief Review, 1955-65,* Progress Publishers, Moscow, 1967.

JANSEN, G.H., *Afro Asia and Nonalighment,* Faber & Faber, London, 1966.

JHANGIANI, M.A., *Jana Sangh and Swatantra : A Profile of the Rightist Parties in India,* Manaktalas, Bombay, 1967.

KARAN, P.P. and JENKINS, W.M., *The Himalayan Kingdoms,* D. Van Nostrand, New York, 1963.

KARUNAKARAN, K.P., *India in World Affairs, 1947-50,* Oxford University Press, 1952.

__________ *India in World Affaris, 1950-53,* Oxford University Press, 1954.

KAUL, B.M., *The Untold Story,* Allied Publishers, Bombay, 1967.

KAVIC, L.I., *India's Quest for Security : Defence Policies,* University of California Press, 1967.

KEY, V.O., *Politics, Parties and Pressure Groups,* Crowell, New York, 1964.

KING-HALL, SIR STEPHEN, *Defence in the Nuclear Age,* Victor Gollan London, 1958.

KISHORE, M.A., *Jana Sangh and India's Foreign Policy,* Associated Publishing House, New Delhi, 1969.

KNORR, KLAUS and VERBA, SYDNEY, *International System – Theoretical Essays,* Princeton University Press, 1961.

KOTHARI, RAJNI, *Politics in India,* Orient Longman, New Delhi, 1972.

__________ (ed.), *State and Nation-Building : A Third World Perspective,* Allied Publishers, Bombay, 1976.

KUNDRA, J.C., *Indian Foreign Policy,* J.B. Wolters, Groningen, 1955.

LAWRENCE, M.W., (ed.), *Neutralism and Nonalignment,* Praeger, New York, 1962.

LEIBENSTEIN, HARVEY, *A Theory of Economic-Demographic Development,* Princeton University Press, 1954.

LINDBLOM, CHARLES, E., *The Policy-making Process,* Prentice-Hall, Englewood Cliffs, 1968.

LEVI, WARNER, *Free India in Asia,* University of Minnesota Press, 1953.

LIDDELL-HART, B.H., *Deterrent or Defence,* Stevens & Sons, London, 1960.

LOHIA, RAMMANOHAR, *Foreign Policy,* P.C. Dwadash Shreni & Co., New Delhi, 1963.

____________ *India, China and Northern Frontier,* Navahind, Hyderabad, 1963.

LONDON, KURT, *The Making of Foreign Policy : East and West,* J.B. Lippincot Co., Philadelphia, 1965.

LYON, PETER, *Neutralism,* Licester University Press, 1963.

MACRIDIS, R.C., *Foreign Policy in World Politics,* Prentice-Hall, Englewod Cliffs, 1967.

MADHOK, BALRAJ, *India's Foriegn Policy and National Affairs* (speeches in parliament), Bharati Sahitya Sadan, New Delhi, 1969.

MANKEKAR, D.R., *Lal Bahadur : A Political Biography,* Popular Prakashan, Bombay, 1968.

MARKEL, L.J. and others, *Public Opinion and Foreign Policy,* Harper & Row, New York, 1949.

MARTIN, L.J., *International Propaganda,* University of Minnesota Press, 1958.

MASANI, M.R., *Why Swatantra?* Popular Prakashan, Bombay, undated.

MASANI, ZAHIR, *Indira Gandhi : A Biography,* Oxford University Press, Delhi, 1978.

MASON, EDWARDS, *Foreign Aid and Foriegn Policy,* Harper & Row, New York, 1964.

MATHAI, M.O., *Reminiscences of the Nehru Age,* Vikas, New Delhi, 1978.

MAXWELL, NEVILLE, *India's-China War,* Penguin Books, 1972.

McMURRY, R. and LEE, M., *The Cultural Approach : Another Way in International Relations,* University of North Carolina Press, 1947.

MENON, K.P.S., *Many Worlds : An Autobiography,* Oxford University Press, 1965.

MENON, V.K. KRISHNA, *India and the Chinese Invasion,* Contemporary Publishers, Bombay, 1963.

MISRA, K.P. *Foreign Policy and its Planning,* Asia Publishing House, Bombay, 1970.

____________ (ed.), *Studies in Indian Foreign Policy,* Vikas, New Delhi, 1969.

___________ (ed.), *Foreign Policy of India : A Book of Readings,* Thomson Press, New Delhi, 1977.

MONTGOMERY, J.D., *Foreign Aid in International Relations,* Prentice-Hall, Englewood Cliffs, 1967.

MORGENTHAU, HANS J., *Politics Among Nations,* Scientific Book Agency, Calcutta, 1966.

___________ *In Defense of the National Interest : A Critical Examination of American Foreign Policy,* Alfred a. Knopf, New York, 1951.

___________ *Dilemmas of Politics,* Chicago University Press, 1958.

MULLIK, B.N., *My Years with Nehru,* 3. vols., Allied Publishers, Bombay, 1971.

MYRDAL, GUNNAR, *Asian Drama,* 3. vols., Allen Lane the Penguin Press, London, 1968.

NAIR, N. PARAMESWARAN, *The Administration of Foreign Affairs in India with Special Reference to Britain,* unpublished Ph.D. dissertation, Indian School of International Studies, New Delhi, 1963.

NEHRU, JAWAHARLAL, *India's Foreign Policy,* Publications Divison, Government of India, Delhi, 1961.

___________ *An Autobiography,* Bodley Head, London, 1943.

___________ *Discovery of India,* Signet Press, Calcutta, 1946.

___________ *Glimpses of World History,* Lindsay Drummond, London, 1938.

___________ *Soviet Russia,* Allahabad Law Journal Press, Allahabad, 1928.

___________ *Before and After Independence* (speeches of Jawaharlal Nehru, 1922-1950), ed. J.S. Bright, Indian Printing Workds, New Delhi, undated.

OVERSTREET, G.D. and WINDMILLER, MARSHALL, *Communism in India,* University of California Press, 1959.

PANIKKAR, K.M., *The Strategic Problems of the Indian Ocean,* Kitabistan, Allahabad, 1944.

___________ *The Future of South-East Asia,* Macmillan, New York, 1948.

___________ *India and the Indian Ocean,* George Allen & Unwin, London, 1951.

___________ *In Two Chinas,* George Allen & Unwin, London, 1955.

___________ *Problems of Indian Defence,* Asia Publishing House, Bombay 1960.

PASSIN, HERBERT, *China's Cultural Diplomacy,* Fraeger, New York, 1963.

PLATT, W., *Strategic Intelligence Production,* Praeger, New York, 1957.

POPLAI, S.I., and TALBOT, PHILIPS, *India and America : A Study of Their Relations,* Indian Council of World Affairs, New Delhi, undated.

POWER, PAUL, F. (ed.), *India's Non-Alignment Policy,* D.C. Heath & Co., Boston, 1967.

___________ *Gandhi on World Affairs,* The Perennial Press, Bombay, 1961.

PRASAD, BIMLA, *The Origins of Indian Foreign Policy,* Bookland, Calcutta, 1960.

PRASAD, EISWESWAR, *The Foundations of India's Foreign Policy, 1860-1882,* Indian Council of World Affairs, New Delhi, 1952.

RAJAN, M.S., *India in World Affairs, 1954-56,* Asia Publishing House, Bombay, 1966.

RAJKUMAR, N.V., *The foreign Department of the Indian National Congress,* AICC, New Delhi, undated (1950?).

RANA, A.P., *The Imperatives of Non-Alignment,* Macmillan, Delhi, 1976.

RANSOM, H.S., *Central Intelligence and National Security,* Harvard University Press, 1958.

RENOUVIN, P. and DUROSELLE, J., tr. MARY ILFORD, *Introduction to the History of International Relations,* Praeger, New York, 1967.

RICHARDS, P.G., *Parliament and Foreign Affairs,* George Allen & Unwin, London, 1967.

ROBINSON, J.A., *Congress and Foreign Policy Making : A Study in Legislative Influence and Initiative,* The Dorsey Press, Homewood, 1962.

ROSENAU, JAMES N. (ed.), *International Politics and Foreign Policy,* Free Press of Glencoe, New York, 1964.

___________ (ed.), *Linkage Politics,* The Free Press, New York, 1969.

ROSINGER, L.K., *India and the United States : Political and Economic Relations,* Macmillan, New York, 1950.

RUSSELL, BERTRAND, *Common Sense and Nuclear Warfare,* Simon & Schuster, New York, 1959.

———— *Power : A New Social Analysis,* Unwin Books, London, 1960.

———— *Justice in War time,* George Allen & Unwin, London, 1917.

SCOTT, A.M. and DAWSON, R.H, (eds.), *Readings in the Making of American Foreign Policy,* New York, 1965.

SIBLEY, M.Q., *The Quiet Battle,* Bharatiya Vidya Bhavan, Bombay, 1965.

SINGHAM, A.W., *The Non-Aligned Movement in World Politics,* Lawrence Hill & Co., Westport, 1978.

SITARAMAYYA, PATTABHI, *History of the Indian National Congress,* 2 vols., Padma Publications, Bombay, 1947.

SNYDER, R.C. and others (eds.), *Foreign Policy Decision-Making : An Approach to the Study of International Relations,* Free Press of Glencoe, New York, 1962.

SOVNANI, N., *International Position of India's Raw Materials,* Indian Council of Word Affairs, New Delhi, 1948.

SPATE, O.H.K., *India and Pakistan : A General and Regional Geography,* Methuen, London, 1960.

STANLEY, JOHN and PEARTON, MAURICE, *The International Trade in Arms,* Chatto & Windus, London, 1972.

SUBRAHMANYAM, K., *The Asian Balance of Power in the Seventies,* Institute for Defence Studies & Analyses, New Delhi, 1968.

SUKHWAL, B.L., *India : A Political Geography,* Allied Publishers, Bombay, 1971.

TAGORE, RABINDRANATH, *Towards Universal Man,* Asia Publishing House, Bombay, 1961.

THIEN, TON THAT, *India and Southeast Asia,* Librairie Droz, Geneva, 1963.

TYABJI, BADR-UD-DIN, *The Self in Secularism,* Orient Longman, New Delhi, 1971.

VAKIL, C.N., *Economic Consequences of Divided India,* Vora & Co., Bombay, 1960.

VENKATASWARAN, R.G., *Cabinet Government in India,* Geoge Allen & Unwin, London, 1967.

VITAL, D., *The Making of British Foreign Policy,* George Allen & Unwin, London, 1968.

WEINER, MYRON, *Party Politics in India,* Princeton University Press, 1957.

WENDZEL, ROBERT L., *International Relations : A Policymaker Focus,* New York, 1977.

WHITAKER, U.G. Jr. *Propaganda in International Relations,* H. Chandler, San Francisco, 1960.

WOLFERS, ARNOLD, *Discord and Collaboration : Essays on International Politics,* Baltimore, 1962.

WOOTTON, GRAHAM, *Interest Groups,* Prentice-Hall, Englewood Cliffs, 1970.

ARTICLES

APPADORAL, A., "India's Foreign Policy", *International Affairs,* January 1949.

__________ "Impact of Federalism on India's Foreign Relations", *International Studies,* July-September 1974.

BAJPAI, G.S., "India and the Balance of Power", *Indian Yearbook of International Affairs,* 1952.

BANDYOPADHYAYA, JAYANTANUJA, "China, India and Tibet", *India Quarterly,* October-December 1962.

__________ "Making of Foreign Policy : A Tentative Subsystemic Model for South Asia", *South Asian Studies,* July 1968.

__________ "The Economic Bases of Foreign Policy", *India Quarterly,* October-December 1969.

__________ "Non-Alignment in India's Foreign Policy", *Indian and Foreign Review,* February 1, 1973.

__________ "The Indian Ocean : Image and Reality", *Seminar,* September, 1974.

__________ "Role of the External Powers in South Asian Affair", *India Quarterly,* October-December 1974.

__________ "International Relations as a Communication System", *International Studies,* April-June 1975.

__________ "Nehru and Non-Alignment", in B.R. Nanda (ed.), *India's Foreign Policy : The Nehru Years,* New Delhi, 1975.

__________ "National Character and Internaional Relations" *International Studes,* October-December 1976.

__________ "Racism and International Relations", *Alternatives,* August 1977.

__________ "Climate as an Obstacle to Development in the Tropics", *International Social Science Journal,* April-June 1978.

__________ "Disarmament and Development : Structural Linkages", *Alternatives,* August 1978.

__________ "The Dynamics of India's Strategic Environment", *International Studies,* October-December 1978.

__________ "India-China Relations : Outlook for the 1980s", *Foreign Affairs Reports,* January 1979.

BEBLER, ALES, "Indo-Pakistan Western Boundary", *India Quarterly,* April-June, 1968.

BARKES, R.N., "India and the Communist World", *Current History,* March 1959.

__________ "India's Ties with the Commonwealth", *Current History,* March, 1963.

BOZEMAN, A.B., "India's Foriegn Policy Today : Reflections upon its Sources", *World Politics,* vol. X, 1957-58.

BRECHER, MICHAEL, "International Relations and Asian Studies, : the Subordinate State System of Southern Asia", *World Politics,* January 1963.

__________ "Elite Images and Foreign Policy Choices", *Pacific Affairs,* Summer 1967.

__________ "Nehru's Foreign Policy and the China-India Conflict Revisited", *Pacific Affairs,* Spring 1977 (review article).

COHEN, B.C., "Foreign Policy-Making : Modern Design", *World Politics,* vol. V, 1952-53.

COHEN, J.B., "India's Foreign Economic Policies", *World Politics,* vol. VII, 1954 55.

DAS GUPTA, A.K., "Impact of Chinese Aggression on India's Economy", *International Studies,* vol. V, July 1963-April 1964.

DE SOLA POOL, "Content Analysis for Intelligence Purposes", *World Politics,* vol. XII, 1959-60.

EVANS, ALLAN,"Intelligence and Policy Formulation, World, Politics, vol. XII, vol. XII, 1959-60.

GANDHI, INDIRA, "India and the World", *Foreign Affairs,* October 1972.

GAUTAM, M., "India's Foreign Policy : the Congress View", *India Quarterly,* January-March 1951.

GHEBHARDT, ALEXANDER, O., "Soviet and US Interests in the Indian Ocean", *Asian Survey,* August, 1975.

GOPAL, S., "India, China and the Soviet Union", *Australian Journal of Politics and History,* August 1966.

GUHA, ASHOK, "India's Foreign Economic Policy", *International Studies,* April 1968.

GUPTA, SISIR, "India and the Soviet Union", *Current History,* March 1963.

__________ "India's Policy Towards Pakistan", *International Studies,* July-October 1966.

"The Power Structure in South Asia", *Round Table* April, 1970.

__________ "Great Power Relations, World Order and the Third World", *Foreign Affairs Reports,* July-August, 1978.

HARRISON, SELIG S., "Troubled India and Her Neighbours", *Foreign Affairs,* January, 1965.

HILSMAN, R., "Intelligence and Policy-Making in Foriegn Affairs", *World Politics,* vol. V, 1952-53.

ILCHMAN, F., "Political Development and Foreign Policy : the Case of India", *Journal of Commonwealth Political Studies,* vol. IV, No. 3, 1966.

JETLY, NANCY, "Parliament and India's China Policy, 1959-1963", *International Studies,* April-June 1976.

KAPUR, ASHOK, "World Politics and the Security of India", *International Journal* Summer 1972.

KARAN, P.P., "India's Role in Geopolitics", *India Quarterly,* vol. IX, No. 2, 1953.

LEVI, WERNER, "Foreign Policy : The Shastri Era", in Misra, K.P. (ed.), *Studies in Indian Foreign Policy,* Vikas, New Delhi, 1969.

__________ "The Elite Nature of New India's Foreign Policy", *Asian Survey,* November 1967.

LYON, PETER, "India's Foreign Policy : Interplay of Domestic and External Factors", *South Asian Studies,* January 1969.

MAHESWARI, S.R., "Informal Consultative Committees of Parliament", *Journal of Constitutional and Parliamentary Studies,* No. 2, 1968.

MAXWELL, NEVILLE, "Jawaharlal Nehru : Of Pride and Prejudice", *Foreign Affairs,* April 1974.

MISRA, K.P., "Foreign Policy Planning Efforts in India", *Institute for Defence Studies & Analysis Journal,* April 1970.

MORGAN, GEORGE ALLEN, "Planning in Foreign Affairs : the State of the Art", *Foreign Affairs,* No. 39, 1690-61.

MORGENTHAU, HANS J., "A Political Theory of Foreign Aid", *American Political Science Review,* June 1962.

MORSE, E.L., "The Transformation of Foreign Policies : Modernization, Interdependence and Externalization", *World Politics,* April 1970.

MUKHERJEE, DILIP, "Decision-Making for Defence", *Institute for Defence Studies & Analyses Journal,* January 1969.

NAIK, J.A., "India's Ruling Janata Party and its Foreign Policy", *Review of International Affairs,* September 29, 1977.

NARAYANAN, K.R., "New Perspectives in Indian Foreign Policy", *Round Table,* October 1972.

PALMER, N.D., "India and the United States : Maturing Relations", *Current History,* March 1959.

———————— "Trans-Himalayan Confrontation", *Orbis,* Winter 1963.

———————— "Foreign Aid and Foreign Policy : the New Statecraft Reassessed", *Orbis,* Fall 1969.

PANIKKAR, K.M., "The Himalayas in India's defence", *India Quarterly,* vol. III, No, 2, 1947.

PARK, RICHARD, "Indian-Ideologies in India's Foreign Relations", *Indian Political Science Review,* January 1977.

RAJAN, M.S., "India and World Politics in the Post-Nehru Era", *International Journal,* vol. XXIV, No. 1, 1968-69.

———————— "India and Pakistan as Factors in Each Other's Foreign Policy", *International Studies,* April 1962.

———————— "India and the Commenwealth", *Australian Journal of Politics and History,* August 1966.

———————— "Chinese Aggression and the Future of India's Non-Alignment Policy", *International Studies,* vol. V, July 1963-April 1964.

RANA, A.P., "The Nature of India's Foreign Policy : An Examination of Indian Non-Alignment in Relation to the Concept of

Balance of Power in the Nuclear Age", *India Quarterly*, April-June 1966.

———— "The Intellectual Dimensions of India's Non-Alignment", *Journal of Asian Studes*, February 1969.

RATNAM, P., "India's Non-Alignment in the 70s", *India Quarterly*, July-September 1970.

ROSTOW, W.W., "The Planning of Foreign Policy", in E.A.G. Johnson (ed.), *The Dimensions of Diplomacy*, Baltimore, 1964.

RUDOLPH, L.I. and S.H., "Generals and Politicians in India", *Pacific Afairs*, Spring 1964.

SCHRADER, ERICH, "Mahatma Gandhi and the Formulation of the Foreign Policy Principles of India", *United Asia*, November-December, 1968.

SINGAL, D.P., "Indian Policy in South-East Asia", *Australian Journal of Politics and History*, August, 1966.

SINGH, HARDIP, "Trade Interests of India and China in the ECAFE Region", *China Report*, May-June 1972.

SOM-DUTT, MAJ-GEN., "The Defence of India's Northern Borders", *India Qurterly*, January-March 1966.

SPROUNT, HAROLD, "Geopolitical Hypotheses in Technological Perspective", *World Politics*, January 1963.

SRIVASTAVA, R.K., "India's West Asia Policy in Perspective", *Afro-Asian and World Affairs*, Spring 1968.

SUBRAHMANYMAN, K., "Ebb and Flow of Power in the Indian Ocean Area", *UNI Journal*, January-March 1968.

———— "The Defence Effort", *Seminar*, October 1968.

———— "Role of Intelligence in National Security", *Institute for Defence Studies and Analyses*, New Delhi, 1968, mimeo.

———— "India's Problems of Security in Retrospect and Prospect", *South Asian Studies*, January 1969.

———— "Decision-Making in Defence", *Institude for Defence Studies and Analyses Journal*, April 1970.

———— "Where Ignorance is Weakess", *The Citizen & Weekend Review*, March 28, 1970.

———— "The Challenge of the Seventies : India's Security", *Institute for Defence Studies and Analyses*, New Delhi, 1970, mimeo.

__________ "Foreign Policy Planning in India", *Foreign Affairs Reports,* January 1975.

DOCUMENTS

An Itemwise Brief on the Activities of the Council, Indian Council for Cultural Relations, cyclostyled, New Delhi, undated (1977?).

Background of India's Foreign Policy (resolutions of the Indian National Congress), ed. N.V. Rajkumar, AICC, New Delhi, 1952.

Both Bread and Liberty, Janata Party Manifesto, New Delhi, undated (1977).

Congress Presidential Addresses, 1911-1934, G. Natesan & Co., Madras, undated.

Constituent Assembly Debates : Official Records, New Delhi, 1947-50.

Constitution of India, Manage of Publications, Government of India, Delhi.

Constitution of the Indian Council for Cultural Relations, Azad Bhavan, New Delhi, undefine (1950).

Documents on Modern Indian Political Thought, 2 vols. ed. A. Appadorai, Oxford University Press, Bombayy, 1976.

Foreign Affairs : A Report to the Congress by the Commission on Organization of the Executive Branch of the Government (Hoover Commission Report), Washington D.C., 1949.

Foreign Policy of India : Texts of Documents, 1947-59, Lok Sabha Secretariat, New Delhi, 1959.

Guidelines on the Consultative Committees of Parliament, Document No. F.1-2/69-CB, dated 23 June 1969, Department of Parliamentary Affairs, Government of India, New Delhi.

India 1947-50 : Selected Documents on Asian Affairs, vol. II, *External Affairs,* ed. S.L. Poplai, Oxford University Press, 1959.

Indian National Congress : Resolutions on Foreign Policy, 1947-50, ed. N.V. Rajkumar, AICC, New Delhi, undated.

Parliamentary Debates : Official Records, New Delhi, 1950-77.

Personnel for the New Diplomacy : Report of the Committee on Foreign Affairs Personnel, (Herter Committee Report), Carnegie Endowment for International Peace 1962.

Policy Statement, Praja Socialist Party, New Delhi, 1956.

Question of Tibet and the Rule of Law, International Commission of Jurists, Geneva, 1959.

Report, Ministry of External Affairs, New Delhi, 1950-51 to 1977-78.

Report of the Commission on the Organization of the Govrnment for the Conduct of foreign Policy (Murphy Commission Report), US Government Printing Press, Washington D.C., June 1975.

Report of the Committee on the Indian Foreign Service (Pillai Committee Report), Ministry of External Affairs, New Delhi, 1966.

Report of the Committee on Representational Services Overseas 1962-63, (Plowden Committee Report) Her Majesty's Stationery Office, London, 1964.

Report of Mr. K.S. Shelvankar on External Publicity, Ministry of External Affairs, New Delhi, 1963.

Report of the Review Committee on Overseas Representation, 1968-69 (Duncan Committee Report), Her Majesty's Stationery Office, London, 1969.

Report of the Officials of the Governments of India and the People's Republic of China on the Boundary Question, Ministry of External Affairs, New Delhi, 1961.

Review of Overseas Representation, Report by the Central Policy Review Staff, Her Majesty's Stationery Office, London, 1977.

Tibet and the Chinese People's Republic : A Report to the International Commission of Jarisis by its Legal Inquiry Committee on Tibet, Geneva, 1960.

Towards a Stronger Foreign Service : Report of the Secretary of State's Public Committee on Personnel (Wriston Committee Report), Washington D.C., 1954.

White Paper : Notes, Memoranda and Letters Exchanged and Agreements Signed Between the Governments of India and China, No. I-VI, Ministry of External Affairs, New Delhi, 1959-61.

Index

D

E

F